Contents

Introduction 3

I. The historical perspective 7

II. The road to the Turkish Republic of Northern Cyprus 20

III. The political kaleidoscope 32

IV. Economic considerations 49

V. The international dimension 55

VI. Conclusions 73

Notes 81

Chronology 94

Glossary 96

Map 1: The Eastern Mediterranean

The Problem of Cyprus

INTRODUCTION

Cyprus presents one of those intractable problems in which bitter historical memory has superseded the desire of its peoples for a harmonious future. Populated largely by Greek-speaking Christians, it was colonized under the Ottoman Empire by Muslim Turks. The two races lived alongside one another in communities scattered throughout the island without ever fully integrating. The Greek-Cypriots outnumbered the Turkish-Cypriots by about three to one and, after the island became a British Crown Colony in 1925, they reasserted their influence. Nationalists sought *enosis*, union of the island with Greece. Irredentist Turks were determined to prevent this. A Greek-Cypriot guerrilla war against the British for *enosis* provoked a militant Turkish-Cypriot campaign for separation of the peoples and partition of the island (*taksim*).

As a compromise, in 1960 the United Kingdom withdrew to Sovereign Base Areas (SBAs) and granted the rest of Cyprus a form of condominium independence which it sought to secure through tripartite treaties of Guarantee and Alliance with Greece and Turkey. The constitutional construct soon fragmented, leading to a short but bitter civil conflict followed by a prolonged period of armed confrontation. The guarantee structure foundered because of the identification of the mainland governments with the interests of their ethnic compatriots rather than with the welfare of Cyprus or its development as a genuine nation state. As all three guarantors were members of the North Atlantic Treaty Organization (NATO), the Alliance, led by its senior partner, the United States, endeavoured to intervene but was rebuffed by President Makarios of Cyprus who feared that this could lead to the dismemberment of Cyprus.

A United Nations peacekeeping force, UNFICYP, arrived on the island in March 1964 and has remained since, seeking to prevent further hostilities, while successive UN Secretaries General have pursued the thankless task of searching for a constitutional formula acceptable to both communities. Every effort at compromise has foundered on old animosities compounded by the machinations of the mainland governments.

In 1974, a military dictatorship in Athens suborned the Greek Cypriot National Guard to stage a coup against Makarios and to install in his stead a unionist president, Nikos Sampson. Turkey responded by invading and occupying the northern third of the island, expelling the Greek-Cypriot residents and concentrating the scattered Turkish-Cypriots in the area, thus achieving its long-standing policy of partition. UNFICYP redeployed in a buffer zone between the two territories. When peace talks broke down in 1975, the UN Secretary General assumed a personal mandate of good offices to continue the search for a new constitutional order for the island. Numerous initiatives have ended in impasse but successive Secretaries General have soldiered on seeking elements of potential compromise. The latest effort, begun in August 1988, provides for the two community leaders, George Vassiliou and Rauf Denktash, to try to achieve agreement through face-to-face negotiations. Secretary General Xavier Pérez de Cuéllar has set an arbitrary time limit of June 1989 for a conclusion to their talks in hopes of imparting a sense of urgency to the need for a successful outcome.

The Turkish-Cypriots have insisted on a loose confederal system which would allow them to continue separate ethnic development. For their security, they have demanded a residual Turkish military presence and some legal device which would ensure Turkey's right of intervention in future. The Greek-Cypriots have sought a form of reunification which would permit refugees to return to their homes. Realizing that while they may be the majority on the island they are a minority in the region, the Greek-Cypriots have searched for guarantees which would secure removal of the Turkish occupation troops and prevent their return.

As the stalemate has dragged on, the Turkish-Cypriots have duplicated all the institutions and infrastructure of a state and, in 1983, declared independence as the Turkish Republic of Northern Cyprus (TRNC). However only Turkey, which provides more than half the budget of the TRNC, recognizes it, though there are indications that its isolation could diminish over time unless there is discernible progress towards a solution to the division of the island.

The inter-communal conflict has had a ripple effect on relations between Greece, Turkey and the UK and has also impinged on other Western institutions; for example, it has been a regular source of friction within NATO. Greece first refused to participate in NATO manoeuvres with Turkey in 1955 because of a dispute over Cyprus. After the Turkish invasion of the island in 1974, Greece protested at what it saw as the ineffectuality of the Alliance to protect the interests of one member against the predations of another by withdrawing altogether from the integrated military structure for a period of six years. Since its reintegration in 1980, there has been a succession of disputes about command-and-control arrangements, assignment of troops, Aegean exercise scenarios, and infrastructure funding which, though strictly Greek–Turkish arguments, had their genesis in the Greek withdrawal from the integrated military structure of the Alliance caused by the Turkish invasion of Cyprus. Greece has not participated in major NATO Aegean exercises since 1983, the year of the Turkish-Cypriot unilateral declaration of independence.

Friction over Cyprus has exacerbated other Greek–Turkish disputes in the Aegean Sea concerning territorial waters, airspace, and continental shelf jurisdiction. Turkey argues that these are purely bilateral issues and bear no relation to the situation on the island, while Greece believes that Turkish diplomatic brokers seek, over the long term, to trade concessions over the island in exchange for advantages in the Aegean. For the first six years of the administration of the Panhellenic Socialist Movement (PASOK) government, which took power in Greece in 1981, Athens refused even to talk to Ankara so long as Turkish troops from the mainland continued to occupy northern Cyprus. The so-called Davos process of *rapprochement* between Greece and Turkey, initiated in the course of 1988, was initially meant to concentrate on bilateral issues but, under the pressure of domestic public opinion, the Greek side has been forced to seek to incorporate Cyprus on the agenda, much to the annoyance of the Turks.

US efforts to resolve the issue of Cyprus, first to impose a settlement and later to aid in the mediation process, have caused adverse reactions in large parts of the electorates of both Greece and Turkey. These reactions have redounded on US military relations with Athens and Ankara and have compromised American dominance of the eastern Mediterranean basin. The Soviet Union has adapted its relations with Greece, Turkey and Cyprus so as to play off one side against the other for its own diplomatic and strategic advantage.

Latterly, Cyprus has become an issue for the European Community (EC). Greece became a full EC member in 1981, Cyprus signed a Customs Union agreement in 1987, and Turkey has made an application for full membership which is currently before the Commission for an opinion. Greece and Cyprus believe that they can persuade the Community that it is impossible to consider Turkish membership so long as Turkish troops continue to occupy northern Cyprus, and they consider that this provides them with their best international leverage in many years to achieve a settlement of the long-standing dispute. The Community, however, has a record of ignoring bilateral disputes between its members.

This Paper traces the history of the inter-communal conflict and catalogues the efforts of the UN to seek resolution. It delineates the political forces on the island and their attitudes towards the national issue, and considers the economic gulf which has grown up between the two communities and its implications for reunification. Finally, the Paper surveys the effects the Cyprus impasse has had on the nexus of relations between Greece, Turkey, NATO, the US, the UK, the Soviet Union and the European Community.

It offers no prescriptions for settlement but does seek to elucidate some of the sensitivities involved in the hope that by this means it might help promote understanding and contribute to resolution of the conflict.

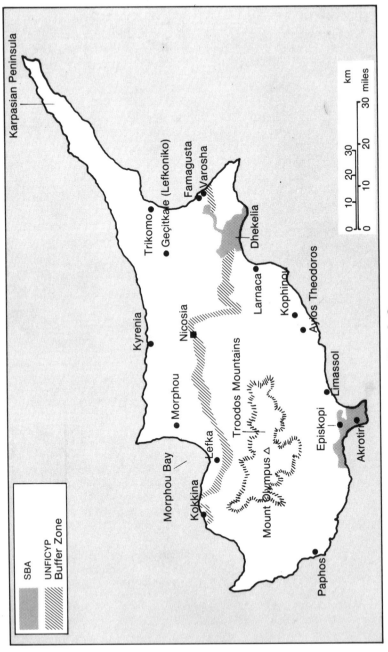

Map 2: Cyprus

Karpasian Peninsula

Trikomo
Geçitkale (Lefkoniko)
Famagusta
Varosha
Kyrenia
Nicosia
Dhekelia
Larnaca
Kophinou
Ayios Theodoros
Morphou
Lefka
Troodos Mountains
Limassol
Morphou Bay
Kokkina
Mount Olympus △
Episkopi
Akrotiri
Paphos

SBA

UNFICYP
Buffer Zone

km
30
20
30 miles
20
10
10
0
0

I. THE HISTORICAL PERSPECTIVE

The colonial period

The island of Cyprus is not important in territorial terms. It is of modest size – 222 kilometres long and 95 kilometres broad at its widest point – with limited agricultural lands and natural resources. Its location, however, is significant. Just 80 kilometres off the south coast of Turkey and 100 kilometres west of the historically turbulent Middle East, it sits astride three major inter-sea routes: the Black Sea to the eastern Mediterranean via the Dardanelles and the Aegean; the western Mediterranean to the Red Sea via the Suez Canal; and, the Mediterranean to the Persian Gulf overland via the Tigris-Euphrates Valley.[1] As a consequence, it has been a magnet for all the imperial powers which have ruled the region. Ethnically Greek since the second millenium BC, Cyprus has been subject in turn to the empires of Assyria, Persia, Macedonia, Egypt, Rome, Byzantium, the Franks and Venice.

In 1571, it was overrun by the Ottomans who installed a substantial garrison, imported settlers from the mainland and encouraged decommissioned soldiers to remain as colonists. These are the ancestors of the current Turkish-Cypriot community.[2]

In 1878, the UK, anxious to protect its sea route to India following Turkish reverses in the war with Russia, impressed an alliance on the Sultan whereby the UK occupied and assumed administration of the island. When Turkey sided with Germany in World War I, the UK annexed Cyprus. The move was formally acknowledged by Greece and Turkey in the Treaty of Lausanne in 1923 and two years later Cyprus became a Crown Colony.

During World War II, Germany had designs on Cyprus as a point of embarkation for an attack on the Suez Canal but the losses sustained in taking Crete dissuaded the Führer from assaulting another large island.[3] Cyprus played no significant role in the war[4] but the fact that it remained in British hands provided insurance against any German seaborne assault in the Middle East. With the airfields at Nicosia and Larnaca reinforced, Cyprus served as a valuable supply and relief station.

Since 1947, the United States with its Sixth Fleet has dominated the sea-lanes of the eastern Mediterranean and, though Cyprus has never been subject to American governance, US policies have had a significant effect on the island's contemporary history. Politically, the modern republic of Cyprus is an independent member of the Non-Aligned Movement but it has been under the influence of NATO since the inception of the Alliance, first as a British colony, and later through the Treaties of Guarantee and Alliance between the UK, Greece and Turkey.

The present division of Cyprus is not, however, the result of exogenous imperial considerations but of indigenous nationalist concerns – albeit complicated by foreign interests and, at times, abetted by them. The partition of Cyprus is the latest separation of peoples arising as a consequence of the creation of the Greek state from former Ottoman territories. The process, begun in the early nineteenth century, sought to consolidate in a Greater Greece the Hellenistic, Orthodox communities scattered throughout the Balkans, the Aegean and Asia Minor. The Cypriots, three-quarters of whom were Greek, also hoped to be incorporated and their aspirations were whetted when the UK offered the island to Greece as an inducement for its support during World War I. The offer was rejected, however, by the pro-German monarch, Constantine I.

Greek expansion ended with the defeat of its army by the Kemalist Turks in Asia Minor in 1922. The Treaty of Lausanne the following year was coupled with a massive population exchange, making refugees of more than a million Greeks and some four hundred thousand Turks.[5] It defined the boundary between the two nations and determined the balance of power between them until 1947 when Italy ceded the Dodecanese islands to Greece, some of which lie just off the Turkish coast.[6]

The Greek-Cypriots continued to press for *enosis* and renewed their claims with vigour in the anti-colonial climate which prevailed after World War II. They advanced their demands under the banner of self-determination, which for a majority was a code word for union. However, the communist party, AKEL (*Anorthotikon Komma Ergazomenou Laou*), the largest organized political force in the island, stopped short of demanding *enosis* because of the persecution of the left in Greece in the wake of the 1947–9 civil war.

The United Kingdom government was principally concerned to preserve its security interests in Cyprus. As it wound down its colonial presence in the Middle East, the UK consolidated many military headquarters in the island and created at Akrotiri its largest operational airfield overseas, which it used in support of its commitments to the Baghdad Pact and later to the Central Treaty Organization (CENTO). Cyprus provided a staging post for flights and fleets in transit to support residual interests in the Far and Near East and, in 1956, served as the launching pad for the British and French intervention in Suez.

On three separate occasions, in 1948, 1954 and 1955, the UK proposed forms of representative government for the island under continued colonial rule. All were rejected by the Greek-Cypriot Ethnarchy Council headed by Archbishop Makarios, and in 1955 a guerrilla campaign in favour of *enosis* was launched by the National Organization of Cypriot Fighters (*Ethniki Organosis Kypriou Agoniston* – EOKA).[7] under the leadership of the fanatical General George Grivas.[8]

Turkey grew ever more concerned about the possibility of another Hellenic island close to its shores. Greece already controlled islands covering the sea routes to all Turkey's Black and Aegean Sea ports. Cyprus lies across the shipping lanes from Mersin and Iskenderun, ports vital for the supply of central Anatolia and the eastern frontier. Although the two states were members of NATO, traditional enmities lay close beneath the surface of the relationship. In any event, some Turks argued, alliances are impermanent and NATO eventually might be dissolved.

Turkey feared that, were the British to withdraw, Cyprus could possibly fall into hostile hands. Ankara already felt exposed to communist danger from the Soviet Union in the north and from Syria, then a Soviet client, in the east. The strength of AKEL led Turkey to believe that an independent Cyprus might accept economic and arms aid from the USSR. Alternatively, were Cyprus to become Greek and were Greece and its islands to be occupied by a foreign power, as had happened during World War II, then Turkey would be virtually encircled.

Ankara decided it required a physical presence on Cyprus.[9] One school of thought argued that the island should revert to Turkish jurisdiction as foreseen in the 1878 treaty; another advanced the idea of establishing a major Turkish military base there. Gradually the notion gained currency of *taksim* and double *enosis*, that is, partition of the island and the unification of the resultant parts with Greece and Turkey respectively.[10] The policy evolved that Turkish-Cypriots should shun contacts with Greek-Cypriots and work towards the creation of an autonomous community.[11] The government of Adnan Menderes sent an official to assist Turkish-Cypriot leader Dr Fazil Küçük in the reorganization of his Cyprus Turkish National Party into the 'Cyprus is Turkish' Party (*Kibris Türktür Partisi* – KTP). The Turkish-Cypriots had their own guerrilla organization *Volkan*.[12] Without Küçük's knowledge, Rauf Denktash, his chief political adviser and principal link with Ankara[13] created an alternative force known as the Turkish Resistance Organization (*Türk Mukavemet Teskilati* – TMT)[14] which superseded *Volkan*. Ostensibly defensive, TMT was also used to harry those Turkish-Cypriots who continued to collaborate with Greek-Cypriots.

Initially, the Greek-Cypriot EOKA forces confined themselves to attacking the UK forces, but the colonial authorities recruited large numbers of Turkish-Cypriots as auxiliary police and, as casualties mounted, so too did inter-communal animosity. In summer 1958, this erupted in a spate of rioting, hostage-taking and killings, prompting the withdrawal of some Turkish-Cypriots from mixed villages into defensive enclaves in larger centres. It coincided with British proposals for a form of government involving Greece and Turkey which would have provided a transition to independence in seven years.[15] This too was rejected by Greek-Cypriot unionists who saw it as the first step along the road towards partition.

The United Kingdom government came to the conclusion that trying to hold the whole of the island was an impossible task, and unnecessary provided it could guarantee its defence interests. The idea gained currency that it 'no longer needed Cyprus as a base but only bases in Cyprus'.[16] Whitehall let it be known that it was prepared to accept any solution on which the Greek and Turkish governments could agree.[17] The 1958 British proposal had convinced Makarios that partition was imminent and prompted him, against the wishes of EOKA, to allow that he would accept independence in lieu of self-determination.

The independent state

In February 1959, the Greek and Turkish Prime and Foreign Ministers negotiated a settlement package, thereafter confirmed by the UK, consisting of three treaties (Establishment, Guarantee and Alliance) plus a complex power-sharing constitution. These Zurich and London Agreements created an independent republic in those parts of Cyprus which were no longer to remain sovereign British territory. Although the Cypriot community leaders attended the London talks, Archbishop Makarios claimed not to have been consulted about certain basic elements of the constitution and only to have concurred in the arrangements under duress.[18] Cyprus reluctantly became an independent state on 16 August 1960.

The Treaty of Establishment provided for two British Sovereign Base Areas (SBAs): Dhekelia, between Larnaca and Famagusta; and Akrotiri, between Limassol and Paphos. They are British Dependent Territories and the Commander British Forces Cyprus is also administrator with executive and legislative authority. Should the UK divest itself of sovereignty, the lands are to be transferred to the Republic.

The Treaty of Guarantee excluded partition or union with any other state and included undertakings by Greece, Turkey and the UK to ensure maintenance of the independence, territorial integrity and security of the Republic, and respect of its constitution. In the event of a breach of any of these conditions, the guarantor powers were to 'consult together with respect to the representations or measures necessary to ensure observance' and, if concerted action was not possible, each reserved the right 'to take action with the sole aim of re-establishing the state of affairs created by the present Treaty'.

Under the Treaty of Alliance, Greece and Turkey were to establish contingents of 950 and 650 men respectively, and these were to join with Cypriot military representatives in a tripartite headquarters to set up and train a 2,000-man Cyprus army. The HQ was to be responsible to a committee of Foreign Ministers of the three contracting parties.

The 199-article constitution created a complex consociational system. All persons (including those who were neither Orthodox nor Muslim) were required to declare themselves to be members of either the Greek community or the Turkish community.[19] The Greek and Turkish languages were to be of equal validity.

– The President of the Republic was to be a Greek-Cypriot, the Vice President a Turkish-Cypriot. Archbishop Makarios became the first president; Küçük the first vice president. Each had powers of veto over laws and decisions of the cabinet or the legislature in key matters.
– The Council of Ministers was to be composed of seven Greek-Cypriot and three Turkish-Cypriot members, with one of the three key posts of defence, finance or foreign affairs always allocated to a Turkish-Cypriot.

- The House of Representatives was to consist of 35 Greek-Cypriots and 15 Turkish-Cypriots elected by their respective communities. Separate majorities were required when votes were taken on vital issues such as the imposition of taxes or duties or modification of the electoral law.
- There were to be Greek and Turkish Communal Chambers, empowered to deal with religious, educational and cultural affairs, and separate municipal authorities for the administration of the respective communities of the five main towns (Nicosia, Limassol, Famagusta, Larnaca, Paphos).
- Posts in the judiciary, civil service, police and gendarmerie were to be apportioned in a 7:3 ratio between the communities, while the army was to be formed in a ratio of 6:4.

The Turkish-Cypriots insisted on interpreting the constitution as a federation, though the term was carefully avoided in the document itself.[20] Makarios feared that it left the door open to partition through the creation of Turkish-Cypriot cantons built round the separate municipal authorities. He claimed that what had been created was a state but not a nation. Certainly the complex of associated treaties severely constrained the sovereignty of the state and did not so much end colonial status as spread it wider through the guarantee of three NATO nations.[21]

Without the utmost goodwill of the two communities, the constitution was a recipe for legal paralysis: inevitably, given the years of strife which had preceded independence, such co-operation was not forthcoming.[22] The structure of an army was created but disputes about its composition meant that it was never fleshed out and irregulars on both sides began to rearm. Perpetual friction in government, coupled with intense pressures on Makarios from disappointed unionists,[23] prompted the Archbishop in November 1963 to propose extensive constitutional amendments which would have removed all Turkish-Cypriot safeguards against domination by the Greek-Cypriots and reduced them virtually to the status of a minority.[24] These were rejected out of hand by the Turkish camp.

On 21 December 1963 fighting broke out between communal militias. In the first few days at least 500 people were killed[25] and thousands wounded; hostages were taken and atrocities committed by both sides. Many Turkish-Cypriots fled their homes and took refuge in the defended enclaves. The Turkish army contingent stationed in Cyprus under the Treaty of Guarantee took up positions commanding the Nicosia-Kyrenia road. Turkish jets buzzed Nicosia, and Ankara threatened an invasion by sea. British troops moved out of the SBAs and established a cease-fire line in Nicosia, known as the Green Line, which has divided the city ever since.[26]

At a conference in London in early 1964, the Greek-Cypriots sought to abrogate the London and Zurich Agreements, particularly the

Treaties of Alliance and Guarantee sanctioning Turkish intervention to uphold Turkish-Cypriot constitutional rights. Instead they proposed a bill of minority rights. The Turkish-Cypriots argued that the fighting confirmed the need for physical separation of the communities and pressed for either partition and a federal state, or partition and double *enosis*. The conference ended in impasse and the fighting continued sporadically until the following August. In the course of that time an estimated 25,000 Turkish-Cypriots, about a fifth of their total numbers, left their homes for the enclaved areas. The Greek-Cypriots cut off communications to them and maintained a blockade of all materials which might be construed as being of military use, including fuel and clothing. This situation prevailed until 1968.

The UK concluded that it could not keep the peace alone and proposed the despatch of an international force consisting of detachments from NATO nations with US logistic support. The US, still unsettled by the assassination of President Kennedy and distracted by its commitments in Vietnam, was reluctant to become involved, although it was perturbed by Makarios' association with the Non-Aligned Movement and by the strength of AKEL. Despite the fact that most of the men in arms were ultra-right-wing nationalists, the Cold War mentality of the day caused policy-makers in Washington to view Cyprus as a potential Mediterranean Cuba, threatening both the south-eastern flank of the Alliance and UK strategic bases on the island. The US concluded that a settlement should be pursued within NATO and not before the UN Security Council, where Soviet influence could be brought to bear. The attitude was summarized by the then US Undersecretary of State George Ball:

> Viewed from Washington, the issues were clear enough. Cyprus was a strategically important piece of real estate at issue between two NATO partners: Greece and Turkey. We needed to keep it under NATO control. The Turks would never give up their intervention rights or be deterred from invading by the interjection of a UN force which they would regard as an instrument of Soviet or Third World politics and subject to manipulation by Makarios.[27]

The US government thus agreed to assume the British mantle as principal diplomatic broker. The catalyst for Washington was an appeal by Makarios for Moscow to deter the embarkation of a Turkish invasion fleet which had assembled at Iskenderun.

The then Supreme Allied Commander Europe (SACEUR), General Lyman Lemnitzer, dissuaded Turkey from sailing, and a scheme was drafted in Washington to despatch a peacekeeping force of 10,000 NATO troops. It was to maintain security for three months while a mediator from a non-guarantor European NATO nation sought a solution.[28] Makarios flatly rejected the proposal and the Soviet leader, Nikita Khrushchev, declared that an attempt to bring Cyprus under the military control of NATO would threaten world peace. US efforts to canvass an alternative were pre-empted by renewed fighting. The Turkish fleet set sail but turned back after appeals by the UK and Cyprus to the UN Security Council.

The UN resolved to despatch a peacekeeping force, the United Nations Force in Cyprus (UNFICYP), and to appoint a neutral mediator.[29] The first detachment of Canadian troops arrived on 14 March 1964 and two intermediaries were nominated, one responsible for the immediate restoration of order, the other charged with seeking a long-term solution.

Ankara continued to make preparations for an invasion to establish a military bridgehead as a basis from which to negotiate a political settlement. A blunt diplomatic note from US President Lyndon Johnson to President Ismet Inonu on 5 June 1964 warned that if Turkish forces intervened and Moscow reacted, then Turkey could not count on NATO support.[30] The incident is widely held to mark a watershed in Turkey's post-World War II commitment to the West and to mark its return to a more accommodating attitude towards its Soviet and Arab neighbours.

Continuing its diplomatic efforts in parallel with the UN, Washington proposed mediation by retired US Secretary of State, Dean Acheson. A formula was devised whereby Greek and Turkish representatives would meet the UN mediator in Geneva, with Acheson available for ancillary talks. The settlement plan proposed by Acheson has never been published officially but several accounts of it have appeared.[31] It envisaged union of Cyprus with Greece and compensation for Turkey in the form of a substantial sovereign territory on the island for military bases,[32] plus cession of the Greek Aegean island of Kastellorizon. Turkish-Cypriots who wished to emigrate would be resettled and compensated; for those who wished to remain on the island there would be three cantons with local administrations under their complete control. An international body would observe the application of human rights, with NATO exercising an enforcement role in the event of violations.[33]

The proposals found a degree of favour with the mainland governments but were resisted by Makarios, and negotiations were broken off after a particularly intensive bout of fighting in August 1964. Greek-Cypriot forces had attacked the Turkish enclave at Kokkina in the north-west in an attempt to stop the import of arms by sea. The Turkish air force retaliated with aerial strikes. Greece was too far away for its air force to respond. Makarios therefore threatened an all-out assault on Turkish-Cypriots throughout the island unless the air attacks ceased. They did, but the ploy proved a propaganda defeat since the Turkish-Cypriots portrayed it as a threat of genocide. Makarios accepted a UN cease-fire and abandoned efforts at a military solution, though he fuelled Western security concerns by contracting with the Soviet Union for the delivery of substantial amounts of armaments, including surface-to-air missiles.[34]

The administration provided for under the constitution had collapsed. During the initial fighting the Turkish-Cypriots' three ministers had withdrawn from government and their representatives had boycotted the House of Representatives. When they sought to return, they were told they had first to accept the constitutional amendments proposed by Makarios in November 1963. They refused. The Greek-Cypriots, arguing that such wilful abstention should not be allowed to undermine the proper functioning of government, invoked the 'doctrine of necessity'[35] and over a period of months introduced the substance of their constitutional amendments as a series of laws. Their irregular forces were reformed as the National Guard, with officers seconded from the Greek contingent under the overall command of a mainland general. Conscription was introduced to bring its strength up to 15,000 men.

To deter a Turkish invasion, 10,000 Greek mainland troops were clandestinely transferred to the island under the command of General Grivas.[36] He was supposed to command only the Greek forces but soon established himself as a *generalissimo* of all the Greek and Greek-Cypriot forces. He considered himself to be answerable only to the General Staff in Athens and not to the Cyprus government. As a consequence, a number of National Guard actions took place without authorization from Makarios.[37]

The Turkish-Cypriots established a parallel hierarchy to govern in the enclaved areas.[38] The political arm, known as the Leadership, consisted of a 13-man General Committee based in Nicosia – including former members of the government, the judiciary and the House of Representatives – plus a series of subsidiary committees at municipal and district level. Government was conducted by the executive decree of Küçük and the district officers. The Communal Chamber continued to function in Nicosia, although its president, Rauf Denktash, who had travelled to the UN to plead the Turkish-Cypriot cause, was barred from returning to the country and spent three years in enforced exile in Ankara.[39] TMT was transformed into a defence force known as the Fighters (*Mücahit*), under Turkish officers from the mainland. The overall commander was a mainland general attached to the Turkish embassy.[40]

An uneasy truce prevailed pending the report of the UN mediator Galo Plaza Lasso in March 1965.[41] It recognized the independent and sovereign nature of Cyprus and ruled out *enosis* or *taksim*. It concluded that the island should be demilitarized, with the question of the British bases to be set aside for further consideration. Most importantly, it stressed that a settlement must be worked out between the two communities. Turkey rejected the report out of hand and called for the resumption of direct negotiations with Greece.

Papandreou's failure to accept Acheson's conditioned *enosis* contributed to the fragmentation of his party and to his being manoeuvred from office in summer 1965.[42] The successor administration under Stefanos Stefanopoulos entered into dialogue with Turkey, and in

December 1966 a regime of 'joint sovereignty' over Cyprus was broached, carefully avoiding the use of the term *enosis*. It would have involved transfer of the Dhekelia SBA to Turkey and 'a special regime of administration and municipalities' for Turkish-Cypriots in areas where they were in the majority.[43] The UK government concurred tentatively but it came to nothing because the Greek government fell while the soundings were still at a relatively early stage.

One of the prime objectives of the Greek Colonels' junta, which seized power in April 1967, was to secure *enosis* '. . . without, however, ignoring the rights of the minority'.[44] The military regime was divided between those who believed union to be a cardinal element of the Greek national birthright and who were prepared, if necessary, to confront Turkey to attain it, and those who felt that a solution could best be achieved by neutralizing Makarios and undertaking direct negotiations with Turkey. The junta leader, George Papadopoulos, anxious to curry favour with the US and NATO, favoured the latter approach.[45] In September 1967, the military regime convoked a summit with Turkish leaders in which the Greek side bluntly proposed *enosis* in exchange for bases in Cyprus for Turkey and NATO, the granting to Turkey of 'a strategic triangular area in Thrace' and 'concessions to the Turkish Cypriots with regard to the domestic regime. . . .'[46] This infuriated Turkey which thought the talks with the Stefanopoulos Government had permanently scotched the demand for *enosis*. The minimum Turkish demand was some form of joint sovereignty. The meeting collapsed in acrimony.

Two months later, more than 20 Turkish-Cypriots were killed after the National Guard launched a massive assault on the villages of Ayios Theodoros and Kophinou in the south of the island – ostensibly to reassert the authority of the Greek-Cypriot police[47] – Ankara mobilized and was only prevented from invading Cyprus by heavy storms. Greece also mobilized and for a fortnight there was a standoff while US presidential envoy Cyrus Vance defused the situation in an exhausting diplomatic shuttle.[48]

The Turkish terms included the withdrawal of Grivas and the 10,000 Greek troops and the dissolution of the National Guard. The Colonels, who could not afford to fight because they had not yet consolidated their control over the armed forces, capitulated. However, after Turkey had stood down its war machine, Makarios reneged and refused to disband the National Guard.

The Turkish-Cypriots, even before the last Greek troops had left the island, declared their Leadership to be the autonomous Provisional Cyprus Turkish Administration. This was approved on 28 December 1967 by an assembly consisting of the members of the General Committee plus other leading former holders of public office. The meeting also ratified a Basic Law, the germ of a constitution, detailing the form of government, administration and judiciary which was to apply in the

Turkish-Cypriot community until such time as the 1960 Constitution would be fully applied.[49]

Inter-communal talks

Archbishop Makarios, who had little sympathy for the dictators in Athens, set aside the pursuit of *enosis* and agreed instead to inter-communal talks for the creation of a new constitutional order for an independent republic. The talks began in June 1968 and continued intermittently for the next six years. They were conducted in secrecy between the conservative Greek-Cypriot politician Glafkos Clerides and Denktash, the pair acting as representatives for their respective community leaders.

Makarios described his new policy as pursuit of the feasible rather than the desirable. The Turkish-Cypriots mistrusted him believing that *enosis* remained his long-term goal. Certainly his pronouncements at the time were ambiguous. The policy divided the Hellenic camp and provoked violent opposition to the Archbishop from both Greek and Cypriot unionists. A group called the National Front embarked upon a campaign of terrorist attacks against public figures who endorsed the policy. There were several assassination attempts against Makarios in which persons closely associated with the Athens junta were implicated.

Greek officers, who were seconded to the National Guard for their loyalty to the junta, bombarded conscripts with propaganda against communists and fellow travellers, among whom they included the Archbishop. Purported plans were uncovered for a *coup d'état* by the National Guard but these were dismissed by Makarios as a forgery. Nevertheless, to preserve his person and position he created a special Tactical Reserve of loyalists within the police force and armed them with Czechoslovak weapons.

Against this backdrop, the inter-communal talks deadlocked in spring 1971 over the degree of political autonomy to be allowed to the Turkish-Cypriots. The government which took office in Ankara after the military *pronunciamiento* in March that year was headed by Nihat Erim, who had been one of the drafters of the 1960 Cyprus constitution. Papadopoulos, leader of the Greek junta, seized the opportunity to make a fresh overture for a negotiated settlement. In May, at a private meeting in the margins of the NATO foreign ministers meeting in Lisbon, the Greek and Turkish governments agreed to promote continuation of the inter-communal talks, but along lines laid down by Athens and Ankara. In exchange for the Turkish-Cypriots accepting a number of Makarios' constitutional amendments, it was proposed that they should have a cabinet minister with extensive authority over local government. Both sides reaffirmed the London and Zurich accords, and Turkey, reiterating its adherence to the Treaty of Guarantee, undertook not to invade Cyprus without prior consultation with Athens.[50] The two governments agreed that if the talks failed to resolve the problem they would act jointly to impose a 'definitive solution' though they apparently differed about the form this might take.

The Graeco-Turkish proposals were rejected by Makarios, who feared that autonomy for the Turkish-Cypriots could ultimately lead to partition. Tension increased, and the prospect loomed of fresh inter-communal fighting. After prolonged wrangling, however, including demands by the Colonels that Makarios recognize Athens as the 'national centre', the situation was finessed by the inclusion of Greek- and Turkish-Cypriot constitutional experts in expanded talks.

To add to the confusion, Grivas, who had been under house arrest in Athens since his recall from Cyprus in 1967, 'escaped' to the island and formed EOKA-B which began a campaign of terrorist acts against supporters of independence. At the time, it was assumed that he had been despatched by Papadopoulos to harry Makarios into compliance with Athens. If the junta really was seeking an accommodation with Turkey, however, logic argues against such an interpretation, since Grivas sought a form of unalloyed *enosis* which was anathema to Turkey. It would seem rather that he had been unleashed by hardliners in the Greek regime who were eventually to gain the upper hand for their policy of settling the Cyprus question by force.

Division of the island
On 25 November 1973, Papadopoulos was overthrown by Brigadier Dimitrios Ioannides, chief of the Military Police. Ioannides was an absolutist who took no position in government but ruled by fiat from the wings. His eight-month tenure was notable for its arbitrariness and the brutal treatment meted out to opponents.

Ioannides had served in Cyprus during the troubles in 1964, and hated both Makarios and the Turkish-Cypriots with almost equal vehemence. The Cyprus coup was planned by the Brigadier's inner circle but approved by the Greek General Staff and executed by the Cypriot National Guard under its Greek commanders.[51] The action took place against a background of confrontation between Greece and Turkey over continental shelf rights and territorial waters in the Aegean. There was a threat of hostilities in Thrace and on the Aegean islands. The Greek General Staff believed that a successful coup in Cyprus, as well as attaining the long-sought objective of *enosis*, would open a diversionary third front.[52]

On 15 July 1974, National Guard forces stormed the Cypriot presidential palace in a bid to kill Makarios. However, the Archbishop managed to escape and made his way abroad with the assistance of British forces via the Sovereign Bases. There was intense fighting between the rebel troops and the police and left-wing irregulars loyal to the Archbishop but the insurgents prevailed and a former EOKA assassin, Nikos Sampson, was installed as president.[53]

Initially, no violence was directed towards the Turkish-Cypriot community and, publicly, Sampson espoused a policy of continued independence. However, his terrorist record and Ioannides' documented hatred of the Turkish-Cypriots caused the minority to fear the worst. Turkey finally seized the opportunity to invade, invoking in justification the Treaty of Guarantee. It styled the intervention a peacekeeping operation designed to secure the safety and constitutional rights of the Turkish-Cypriots.[54]

Before intervening unilaterally, Prime Minister Bulent Ecevit spent 48 hours in London seeking to persuade the Labour government of Harold Wilson to co-operate in some form of joint action such as a Turkish landing via the SBAs or under British air cover. The UK was prepared to undertake only diplomatic initiatives and sought to convene talks among the guarantors. Ecevit refused to meet the Greek representatives, claiming that by staging the coup they had forfeited their guarantor status.[55] Ioannides was equally intransigent and refused to participate either in tripartite talks or in a bilateral meeting with UK government representatives.[56] The junta assumed that the US and NATO would not allow Turkey to invade Cyprus and, indeed, US Assistant Secretary of State for Near Eastern and South Asian Affairs, Joseph Sisco, did embark on a frantic shuttle between Athens and Ankara in an effort to prevent the invasion.[57]

It seems unlikely, however, that Ecevit, presiding over a tenuous coalition, could have contained the Turkish General Staff even had he wanted to. The Turkish military had felt humiliated by being forced to stand down in 1964 and 1967 and knew there would never be another opportunity providing the same justification as the situation which prevailed in the wake of the Greek-sponsored coup.

Turkish tactics envisaged a two-stage operation: first to establish a beachhead, then, following consolidation, to occupy a substantial zone in the north. The initial assault, over the period 20–22 July 1974, secured limited territory around the north coast town of Kyrenia and a corridor to the enclaved sector of north Nicosia. In the first wave some 6,000 men with 30 tanks were landed by sea and parachute drop. They met much stiffer resistance than anticipated and were confined within vulnerable positions. Ankara, therefore, accepted a UN appeal for a cease-fire.[58]

The action caused the Greek Chiefs of Staff finally to confront the junior officers who had run Greece since 1967. On 23 July, the senior officers turned over power to the former politicians, and on 24 July a national unity government was sworn in under the conservative Constantine Karamanlis. In Cyprus, Glafkos Clerides took over as President.

British Foreign Secretary James Callaghan convened talks between the governments of the guarantor powers in Geneva from 25–30 July.[59] These were followed by an expanded meeting involving Clerides and Denktash over the period 9–14 August. Initially, both the Turks and the Turkish-Cypriots demanded a bizonal federation with a northern territory, comprising 34 per cent of the island, autonomous in law and internal administration. Under pressure from the US, Ankara agreed to a compromise formula involving the establishment of six Turkish-Cypriot cantons, each with access to the sea, one comprising 17 per cent of the territory of the island. Denktash, however, continued to insist on a bizonal solution and, ultimately, Ankara reverted to this position. Neither the Greek nor the Greek-Cypriot governments, with their tenuous hold on power, could accept such a solution for fear of being overthrown by chauvinist extremists.

Despite having accepted the cease-fire, Turkey had reinforced its troop concentration and engaged in a series of advances to make its bridgehead more viable. It used the hiatus afforded by the talks to muster for a second advance. Callaghan has written that he believed the Turkish delegate, Foreign Minister Turan Gunes, 'used stalling tactics merely to gain time and prevent progress'.[60] Between 14–16 August, some 40,000 men[61] with 200 tanks poured through the Kyrenia salient and other landing points to seize 37 per cent of Cyprus north of a 180-kilometre line running from Famagusta in the east to the Morphou Bay on the north-west coast. (See map on p. 6.)

Karamanlis proposed to send Greek submarines and aircraft to Cyprus to help defend the island but was advised by the Chiefs of Staff that such operations were impossible.[62] To assuage furious Greek public opinion, he ordered the withdrawal of Greek forces from the NATO integrated military command. It was hoped that the price for Greece's return would be concessions towards a settlement.[63]

Ioannides' strategy in launching the coup has been the subject of speculation. Received wisdom among Greeks and Greek-Cypriots is that he expected a Turkish response and was prepared to see Ankara establish a limited military presence on the island in exchange for *enosis*. There is indirect evidence for this. Late on 20 July, half a day into the first Turkish action, Greek foreign ministry staff canvassed Western diplomats in Athens for support for an extraordinary UN Security Council session to secure a cease-fire. They said that Ioannides was prepared to see the estimated 6,000 Turkish invasion troops remain in Cyprus, provided they withdrew to the Turkish enclaves.[64] This would have created a situation similar to that conceived by Acheson in 1964. Turkey, however, was determined upon a more decisive resolution – *de facto* partition.

Did Ioannides believe he had Turkish agreement to this limited response scenario? It has been reported that a former CIA station chief in Cyprus met Sampson and other EOKA-B figures in Athens in February 1974 and that shortly before the *putsch* a veteran Greek-American CIA operative conferred with Ioannides.[65] It is conceivable that, in the labyrinth of conspiracies which surrounded the Colonels' dictatorship, Ioannides convinced himself that he had reached an arrangement satisfying both his own aspirations and those of other members of the Western alliance who wished to see Cyprus out of the non-aligned fold and secure within the West. Ironically, the result was to create a permanent source of friction between Greece and Turkey and this has caused disruption on the south-eastern flank.

II. THE ROAD TO THE TURKISH REPUBLIC OF NORTHERN CYPRUS

At the cessation of hostilities in 1974, there were two cease-fire lines separated by a buffer zone which ran from Famagusta in the east to Morphou Bay in the north-west of the island. This zone ranged in width from just 20 metres at points in central Nicosia up to seven kilometres in open countryside and comprised some three per cent of the territory of the island. UNFICYP redeployed into this area to stand between the combatants.

Separation of peoples

The Turkish-Cypriots were intent on segregating the communities while the Greek-Cypriots sought to restore the heterogeneous distribution of population by preventing the movement of settled communities and pressing for the safe return of refugees to their homes. Some 160,000 Greek-Cypriots had fled before the Turkish advance, leaving only 20,000 Greek-Cypriots in the northern territory, while 40,000 Turkish-Cypriots remained south of Greek-Cypriot lines, a fifth of them sheltering at Episkopi in the western SBA. Under intense diplomatic pressure by Ankara, the UK government allowed the latter group to be airlifted to the north via Turkey. Greek-Cypriot police used force to restrain other Turkish-Cypriots attempting to move to the northern territory, while Turkish troops and irregulars intimidated Greek-Cypriots to leave. Within a year the numbers of those remaining outside of their respective communities had dwindled to some 10,000 on either side.

Coercion by the Turkish-Cypriots, including threats of a further Turkish advance to rescue their compatriots, finally resulted in an agreement, in August 1975, whereby the balance of the Turkish-Cypriots were allowed to travel north in an organized programme. In exchange for this, the residual Greek-Cypriots were to be given the option of leaving or continuing to live in their homes, with no restrictions on their movements and with facilities for education in Greek and for the practice of the Orthodox religion. UNFICYP was to monitor this process.[1]

Turkish-Cypriot political leaders styled this a 'population exchange agreement' although the Greek-Cypriots' intention was quite the contrary, namely that it should establish the principle that their people had a right of residence in the north with amenities to sustain them.[2] In the course of the succeeding year, Greek-Cypriot numbers in the north dwindled to 3,600. The UN complained that the agreed procedure for screening applicants for transfer to establish whether they were leaving of their own volition had not been implemented. By mid-1988 a mere 652 Greek-Cypriots remained in the northern territory.[3]

Introduction of settlers

A programme was instituted to settle mainland Turks in the north of the island. The majority were poor, landless peasants who were used to supplement the manual labour force as farm-hands and construction workers. Those who remained five years, or who married locals, have been granted citizenship by the Turkish-Cypriot authorities, although the Greek-Cypriots contest its validity. Citizenship was also offered to Turkish soldiers who had served in Cyprus prior to 1974, and to the families of soldiers who had become casualties during the invasion. The progeny of these people, being born on the island, are entitled to Cypriot citizenship, even in Greek-Cypriot eyes.

The Greek-Cypriots accuse the Turkish-Cypriots of seeking to change the demographic structure of the island. Whereas at separation the Turkish-Cypriots numbered about 120,000, some 18 per cent of a population of 650,000, they now number some 165,000 or 24 per cent.[4] The Turkish-Cypriot leadership says no more than 14,000 mainlanders have been granted citizenship, and that the growth in the size of their community has largely been due to the return of Turkish-Cypriots who had emigrated during the years of troubles.[5] The Greek-Cypriots allege that there have been 65,000 settlers from the mainland,[6] and that the reason this figure is higher than the difference between the number at the time of separation and the current level is because there has been substantial emigration by indigenous Turkish-Cypriots who do not care for the quality of life under military occupation or for the society of their new mainland neighbours.[7]

Certainly the immigrants have created friction. They have generally been poorer, less well educated and more religiously rigorous than their Turkish-Cypriot counterparts. They have been prepared to work for lower wages and thus have put a brake on income growth. One example of cultural alienation cited by Turkish-Cypriots has been the reintroduction (albeit on a limited scale) of Muslim polygamy. The average family size among settlers is said to be five and, if the higher immigration estimates are valid, then mainlanders could eventually dominate the north.

Status of territories

In September 1974, the Turkish-Cypriot provisional administration restyled itself as the Autonomous Cyprus Turkish Administration. The following February, the northern territory was declared to be the Turkish Federated State of Cyprus (TFSC). The Turkish-Cypriots presented it, not as a breakaway state, but as a potential constituent of a future federated Cyprus. However, at the same time that they have participated in protracted negotiations for a federal government, they have simultaneously created all the institutions of an independent state: constitution, executive, legislature, central bank,[8] courts, police and army. In November 1983, Denktash declared the territory to be the independent Turkish Republic of Northern Cyprus (TRNC). Turkey is the only nation to recognize it.

The United Nations, its member governments (apart from Turkey) and other international agencies continue to recognize the Greek-Cypriot government as the legitimate government of the Republic. During the decade 1964–74 the Greek-Cypriot government did exercise nominal jurisdiction over the whole of the island, though its writ did not run in the enclaves and, even elsewhere, could sometimes only be exercised through the use of force. Since the invasion, it has had no effective authority in the northern territory, however, it has utilized its international recognition to interdict communication and commerce. It has persuaded international air, maritime, postal and telecommunication authorities not to deal directly with the Turkish-Cypriot administration, and all these services have had to be routed through Turkey.

Export trade from the north has been disrupted by court challenges arguing that the produce has been 'stolen'. Objections have been raised within the EC about Turkish-Cypriot export documentation. Vessels known to have called at northern ports have been arrested if they ventured into southern waters. Passports have been refused and diplomatic initiatives undertaken to prevent international recognition of Turkish-Cypriot travel documents. To visit most countries, Turkish-Cypriots must acquire a Turkish passport. Foreigners found to have entered the island via northern ports have faced a threat of prosecution for illegal entry. Tourists have been allowed to visit the north on day passes but not permitted to stay overnight.

The cumulative effect of these measures has been to prevent the growth of a viable economy in the north. Ironically, rather than forcing the Turkish-Cypriots to consider reintegration, it has reinforced separatist tendencies by making their community ever more dependent on Turkey for its sustenance.

Perceptions of federation
Efforts to achieve a settlement have foundered on the two communities' diametrically opposed conceptions of the basic constitutional structure. The Turkish-Cypriots have argued that, as there is no valid central authority to devolve power to the regions, there should be a loose form of confederal government with powers assigned to it by the regions. If the system worked then other functions might be delegated to the central authorities later. They describe the process as federation by evolution. They have insisted on no dilution of their community by the return of Greek-Cypriots to homes in the north in the near future and no substantial reduction in the size of their territory. Above all they have insisted that there must be a continued Turkish security guarantee, including a troop presence on the island, and a continued legal right of unilateral intervention by Turkish armed forces.

The Greek-Cypriots, for their part, have reluctantly accepted that the settlement should be based on a bi-regional federation, but have sought to assert the primacy of the central government and to ensure that it would not be immobilized by a lack of problem-solving mechanisms as it was in 1963. They have insisted on the eventual return of displaced persons and on the implementation of three basic freedoms: the rights of ownership of property, settlement, and freedom of movement. They have demanded withdrawal of Turkish troops and settlers and argued that, if any security guarantee is necessary, it should be provided by members of the international community and not by the mainland governments.

The negotiating process

In November 1974, the UN General Assembly voted unanimously for a resolution acknowledging that the constitutional make-up of Cyprus was a matter for the two communities meeting 'on an equal footing'.[9] The resolution called for a speedy withdrawal of all foreign forces, an end to foreign interference and the return of refugees to their homes. Early contacts between Denktash and Clerides concentrated on the exchange of prisoners of war and other humanitarian issues, but they also touched upon the possibility of a peace agreement involving a bizonal federation. The *quid pro quo* for acceptance of the division would have been Turkish handover of the abandoned Varosha area of Famagusta and a withdrawal of Turkish forces from the orchards of Morphou, in the north-west, and a portion of the arable Mesaoria plain, in the centre of the eastern district. This would have allowed about half of the Greek-Cypriot refugees to return to their homes. According to press reports at the time, the Greek-Cypriots were prepared to see the Turkish-Cypriots maintain about a quarter of the island while the Turkish-Cypriots demanded around a third.[10]

Any possibility of an early settlement ran aground, however, when Archbishop Makarios returned to the island in December 1974. While he acknowledged the territorial division, he inclined to rhetoric about a long struggle through the UN and other international fora to deny the Turks the fruits of their aggression.[11]

Contacts between the two sides were broken off following the February 1975 declaration of the TFSC but resumed after a fresh Security Council resolution which called upon the Secretary General to undertake a new mission of good offices.[12] Talks were reconvened in late April 1975 and have continued intermittently since. Venues have included Vienna, London, New York and Nicosia. Various procedures have been adopted, including direct talks between delegated negotiators and indirect proximity talks in which UN officials have had discussions with representative officials and then relayed their findings to the UN Secretary General for collation. There have also been several summit meetings between community leaders.

High-level agreements

The first meeting between the then leaders of the two communities, Makarios and Denktash, took place in February 1977, and produced a Framework Agreement which set the parameters for all subsequent negotiations.[13] It said that Cyprus would become a bi-communal, federal republic; that the powers and functions of the federal government should be such as to safeguard the unity of the country; that a territorial settlement should take account of productivity, economic viability and land ownership; and, that the three freedoms (freedom of movement, settlement and property ownership throughout the country) were open to discussion, taking into account 'certain practical difficulties which may arise for the Turkish-Cypriot community'.

However, the specific proposals which flowed from this agreement highlighted the gulf between the two sides, first at talks in Vienna in March 1977, and, later, in a document produced by the Turkish-Cypriots in April 1978. At the Vienna meeting, the Greek-Cypriots submitted a map which acknowledged that the federation should consist of two regions but which limited Turkish-Cypriot territory to just 20 per cent of the island behind a convoluted boundary.[14] Its contours, the Greek-Cypriots argued, would put the properties of 120,000 of their refugees within the southern zone. The remainder could then settle in the north without swamping the Turkish-Cypriots. The Greek-Cypriots proposed a strong central government which would have sole authority to make international agreements.

The Turkish-Cypriots, on the other hand, proposed a constitutional structure which constituted a form of sovereignty association.[15] The two states would delegate certain powers to the federal government, a purely representational presidency would be held in rotation, and executive powers would be vested in the presidents of the federated states. Defence was to be 'secured by the land forces of each Federated State conjointly' and, though foreign affairs was to be a federal responsibility, the states would have powers to enter into agreements with foreign governments 'particularly, their respective motherlands'.

The Turkish-Cypriots suggested six minor adjustments to the cease-fire lines and said that the territory of the buffer zone should be 'included in these readjustments'. It also was allowed that Greek-Cypriots might return to the Varosha district of Famagusta. This was a concession of some substance as the resort area, which at the time of the invasion included the majority of the hotels on the island, had been home to some 30,000 Greek-Cypriots. The Turkish-Cypriots insisted, however, that the area should remain under TFSC jurisdiction.

President Makarios died in August 1977 and there was a hiatus while his successor Spyros Kyprianou established himself in office. He met briefly with Denktash in January 1978 but dismissed out of hand the Turkish-Cypriot negotiating proposals. It was not until May 1979 that these two men were to have substantive talks.

In the interim, the US, in conjunction with the UK and Canada, advanced a settlement package sketching a unitary government with forms of power-sharing and mechanisms to resolve deadlock.[16] It proposed that the Turkish-Cypriots should make 'significant' geographical adjustments and that non-Cypriot troops should withdraw 'except for those specifically agreed'. It called for refugees who wished to return to their homes to be allowed to do so but acknowledged that a proportion might not wish to. They could receive a settlement from a 'reconciliation fund' to which foreign governments and aid agencies might contribute. It said Varosha should be resettled under UN auspices. The Greek-Cypriots objected to the constitutional arrangements, while the Turkish-Cypriots rejected its suggestions on territory and security. Both sides were suspicious of the provenance of the proposals and they were allowed to lapse.

At their May 1979 meeting, Kyprianou and Denktash agreed upon a ten-point memorandum which refined and elaborated upon the 1977 Framework Agreement.[17] But talks based on this agreement foundered within a week on questions of security, and it took more than a year of intense consultations by UN Secretary General Kurt Waldheim and his representatives to get them restarted.

The format involved delegated negotiators meeting under the auspices of the Secretary General's special representative, Hugo Gobbi, with periodic UN 'evaluations' of their progress. The evaluation of November 1981, which was later to attract renewed attention, spoke of a federation comprising two provinces and a federal district with two administrative districts making up the northern province and four in the south.[18] It made reference to a Federal Council comprising one representative from each administrative district, coupled with a six-member Federal Government. The Council would be responsible for setting the policy of the government and allocating the federal budget, though the powers of the government were not spelled out. It referred to a Chamber of Provinces in which each community would have ten members, and a Popular Chamber with one member for each 10,000 of the population. There were no details of how this structure would function.

During the course of these talks, which dragged on for a further 250 sessions until suspended in April 1983, the impression grew among Greek-Cypriots that the Turkish-Cypriots were merely spinning out the process while consolidating their grip on the northern territory. The Turkish-Cypriots for their part, grew increasingly frustrated at the Greek-Cypriot unwillingness to treat them as equals.

The election of the Panhellenic Socialist Movement (*Panellinio Sosialistiko Kinima* – PASOK) to power in Greece in October 1981 heightened tensions. PASOK policy was that Cyprus was not so much an inter-communal problem as an international issue of invasion and occupation. The new Greek prime minister, Andreas Papandreou, said he supported dialogue to resolve domestic Cypriot issues but also advocated an international conference to deal with the international aspects. He promised a 'crusade . . . to mobilize internationally all the sources which could contribute to the promotion of a fair Cyprus solution'.[19] Following a visit to the island by Papandreou in January 1982, the first ever by a serving Greek Prime Minister, Greek-Cypriot willingness to make concessions noticeably waned.

Each year between 1974 and 1979, the government of the Republic ritually returned to the winter session of the UN General Assembly seeking a further resolution calling for a settlement. This had the effect of buttressing Greek-Cypriot authority as the legitimate government of the island. During the course of the talks (1980–83), the procedure was suspended. In May 1983, however, a new resolution was sought, not directly by the Cyprus government, but through the intermediation of a contact group of non-aligned nations. Nevertheless, it incorporated all the Greek-Cypriot concerns and, moreover, resurrected the concept of an international conference. Denktash claimed that this constituted a refusal to recognize the equality of the Turkish-Cypriots and broke off the talks, asserting that the only way he would secure parity with the Greek-Cypriots was to declare independence.[20]

In an urgent effort to try to resume the negotiations, the Secretary General presented the parties with an *aide-memoire* in which he selected a number of key issues – including territorial concessions by Turkey, a presidency which would rotate between the two communities, a central federal government and a power-sharing administration – and proposed alternative solutions couched in such a way as to define the gap between the two sides and promote further negotiation. The initiative prompted a crisis in the Greek camp. Kyprianou and Papandreou reacted negatively, while the Greek president Constantine Karamanlis urged acceptance as a basis for negotiation. When Kyprianou finally replied in September, he said he accepted the methodology of the Secretary General but not the substance of his proposals. The response created divisions in the alliance between Kyprianou's minority ruling party and the communists who had helped return him to power in the February 1983 elections. Nicos Rolandis, who had served as Foreign Minister for the previous six years, resigned, claiming that Kyprianou had mishandled, and probably scuttled, the UN initiative. Denktash demanded that Kyprianou should meet him face-to-face by the end of October, failing which he would go through with his threat to declare independence.

UDI and its aftermath
On 15 November 1983, the TFSC was unilaterally transformed into the independent Turkish Republic of Northern Cyprus (TRNC). The move was made during the interregnum in Turkey between the election and the taking of office of Prime Minister Turgut Ozal, the unexpected victor in the elections which ended the tri-service dictatorship (1980–83). Ankara claimed to have been taken by surprise, though on 14 October 1983 Denktash had publicly declared his intention of making

the move precisely at this time. 'I want', he said, 'to declare independence before this present government [in Turkey] goes out and before the new government comes in so they are not accused of having done it themselves – and they have not consented to it, they don't know that I have the intent. I am now disclosing it'.[21] Ankara recognized the new state immediately and the following year exchanged ambassadors.

The unilateral declaration of independence (UDI) galvanized the new UN Secretary General Xavier Pérez de Cuéllar, (Waldheim's successor) to new efforts. He proposed to collate all the elements of consensus from the years of negotiation into a Draft Agreement and to couple this with a mechanism for resolution of outstanding issues. The draft would be signed on the understanding that the results would be considered as an integrated whole, that is, that the ultimate commitment to an overall solution would depend upon resolution of all issues to the mutual satisfaction of both sides.[22]

The process began in late 1984 with so-called proximity talks between representatives of the Secretary General and the communities and culminated in a much-fanfared summit between the communal leaders at UN headquarters in New York from 17 to 20 January 1985. This last involved at least four meetings between Kyprianou and Denktash, but, in the end, the summit foundered on the issue of whether the text, which was couched in general terms with substantial lacunae, should be signed before or after further negotiations. Denktash insisted that it must be signed before the negotiations recommenced, arguing that the concept of viewing the agreement as an integrated whole guaranteed the Greek-Cypriots' right to reject its contents if they did not like the final outcome. Kyprianou, on the other hand, insisted on prior negotiations, arguing that the text was too vague and that public opinion would not permit the Greek-Cypriots to go back on an agreement once they had already signed it.

It was not the Secretary General's intention that the document should be signed without discussion, but he obviously had been over-optimistic about what could be achieved in four days of talks. The Greek-Cypriot refusal to sign left a public impression that they were responsible for the failure of the summit. Their diplomatic advantage declined and Kyprianou subsequently adopted a defensive posture. He returned to Cyprus to censure in the House of Representatives.

Pérez de Cuéllar, 'being convinced that the gap between the two sides had never been so narrow',[23] pressed ahead with a revised Draft Agreement which the beleaguered Kyprianou agreed to sign. Denktash, who had suspended development of the institutional structure for the independent TRNC while the Secretary General's initiative was in train, declined to acknowledge this and pressed on with the creation of a new constitution and with fresh presidential and parliamentary elections. Nevertheless, in August 1985, without conceding that he was negotiating the Draft Agreement, he sent the Secretary General a detailed critique of the revision.

The Draft Framework Agreement

The two sides allowed that the Secretary General should again consolidate existing texts and produce a further document. This Draft Framework Agreement was presented on 29 March 1986.[24] It is indicative of the self-perpetuating nature of the problem that this document outlined a government structure similar to that contained in the 1960 constitution, but with even greater potential for impasse.

- There were to be two provinces or federated states competent in all matters not assigned to the federal government. The central government's responsibilities were to be: foreign affairs; federal financing (including taxation and customs duties); monetary and banking affairs; federal economic affairs; (including trade and tourism); posts and telecommunications; international transport; natural resources; federal health and veterinary matters; trading standards; federal judiciary; appointment of federal officers; federal security and defence. However, ten of these were to be designated matters of special concern to the Turkish-Cypriots and hence subject to special voting procedures.
- The president was to be Greek-Cypriot and the vice president Turkish-Cypriot, each with rights to veto laws or decisions of the Council of Ministers or the legislature in agreed areas – 'it being understood that the scope will exceed that covered by the 1960 constitution'.
- The Council of Ministers was to consist of seven Greek-Cypriots and three Turkish-Cypriots with discussions to consider guaranteeing the post of Foreign Minister to a Turkish-Cypriot. For any law to pass the Council in one of the 10 special categories there would have to be 'weighted voting' – a simple majority including at least one Turkish-Cypriot vote.
- The bicameral legislature was to have a lower chamber with Greek and Turkish representation in a ratio of 7:3 and an upper chamber where they would be represented equally. Adoption of legislation in the areas of special concern to the Turkish-Cypriots would require majorities of each community's representation in both chambers.
- There was to be complex deadlock-resolving machinery, including conciliation committees drawn from the legislature and *ad hoc* expert committees. Any contested matter could also be put to a referendum among the members of the community opposing it. A Constitutional Court would rule on whether bills were compatible with the charter or discriminated against a community. It was also to adjudicate disputes relating to distribution of powers and functions.

Outstanding matters of territorial adjustment, troop withdrawals, security guarantees and the 'three freedoms' would be dealt with through a two-tier negotiating process. Every three to four months the Secretary General would convene a high-level meeting for which he would set the agenda. The community leaders or their delegates would review the work of, and give guidance to, working groups which would be responsible for elaborating details.

It was agreed that at mutually acceptable dates the Varosha district of Famagusta and six other areas would be placed under UN jurisdiction for resettlement, and Nicosia airport would be re-opened under UN auspices with free access for both sides. It was also agreed that there should be territorial adjustments, though here the two sides differed. The text to which the Greek-Cypriots had agreed said that the Turkish-Cypriot province should be 'of the order of 29 per cent' while the final text, approved by the Turkish-Cypriots, said it should be 'in the order of 29+ per cent'.

The three freedoms were to be discussed in the light of 'certain practical difficulties' for the Turkish-Cypriot community. The Turkish-Cypriot leadership have given different interpretations to this, depending upon the prevailing political climate. When relaxed, they have suggested that, in principle, Greek-Cypriots should continue to be allowed to own property in the north with the eventual possibility of settlement once good relations were established, always provided that the number of people who returned did not eliminate the Turkish-Cypriot majority. Freedom of movement would be total, except for a small blacklist of known EOKA terrorists. As short a period as five years for the process to commence has been mentioned.

At times of tension, however, attitudes have hardened. During one such period, Denktash suggested in a private interview that the only Greek-Cypriots who would be allowed to return to the north would be those who were economically useful. They would be licenced to enter to work but not to reside. He implied that there would be a settling of accounts regarding property and an end to all question of resettlement. Other officials have implied that there might not even be a settlement of land claims.

Both the text agreed by the Greek-Cypriots in 1985 and that agreed by the Turkish-Cypriots in 1986 spoke of the setting of a timetable for the withdrawal of non-Cypriot troops and for the establishment of 'adequate' guarantees: the text agreed by Kyprianou said 'in connection with international treaties' which could have been taken to exclude a role for the traditional guarantor powers, while the final text accepted by Denktash specified 'in connection with the treaties of guarantee and of alliance', implying continuation of a legal right of unilateral intervention for Turkey.

The March 1986 document, although in many respects similar to that agreed by Kyprianou a year earlier, contained enough variations to lead the Greek-Cypriots to see the negotiating process being prolonged indefinitely. Moreover, they felt that, having made extensive concessions on constitutional matters, they had got nothing in return on security and territory. The concept of the integrated whole was an insufficient guarantee that their concerns would be satisfied. The Greek-Cypriots' sole negotiating leverage lay in the fact that they continued to be the internationally recognized government. Hence they wanted prior assurances that, were they to abandon this status and enter into a transitional government charged with implementation of a settlement, Turkey would not find some pretext for halting the timetabled withdrawal of its troops.[25] Kyprianou proposed two alternative courses of action, either an international conference to deal with the withdrawal of troops and settlers and with guarantees, or a further high-level meeting to discuss these matters together with the application of the three freedoms.

Denktash accepted the Secretary General's document on the conditions that the Greek-Cypriots lifted their economic embargo and that the Secretary General did not attempt to force the pace of negotiations. But he insisted that he was not prepared to negotiate Turkey's guarantee which he described as 'the *sine qua non* condition for the security and survival of the Turkish-Cypriot people'. He insisted that it must be maintained in both 'law and practice'.[26]

Pérez de Cuéllar made repeated overtures to get the two sides talking again, but the impasse continued with Kyprianou becoming increasingly defensive and Denktash ever more truculent. Positions hardened even further after Ozal visited the island in July 1986 and commented that he felt as if he 'were in a province, town or village in Turkey' and urged the Turkish-Cypriots 'to transform the north of Cyprus into one of the greatest countries in the world'.[27]

Matters remained stalemated until February 1988 when Kyprianou was defeated in the presidential elections by George Vassiliou. Within three months of taking office, Vassiliou had agreed in principle to enter into face-to-face negotiations with Denktash. The Secretary General proposed discussions between the two community leaders based on the high-level agreements of 1977 and 1979 with a target date of June 1989 for a settlement.

Following a visit to Ankara, Denktash dropped his insistence on the March 1986 document as the sole basis for a settlement and agreed to talks. He demanded that three other documents be included as a basis for discussion, including the UN 'evaluation' of November 1981 with its structure based on a 4:2 ratio in the executive and the provincial and federal chambers.[28] Denktash and Vassiliou had a preliminary meeting in Vienna in late August 1988 and negotiations began in September.

The stance of the two communities

In the north, Denktash and conservative politicians favouring separatism have been sustained in office, largely by democratic means, although on occasion by the coercion of such domestic opposition as exists. The result has been that there has been no hint from the north of any preparedness to seek accommodation or compromise.

Denktash has little to gain from a settlement and therefore scant incentive to make concessions. The Turkish military have imposed *de facto* partition and forced division of the Cypriot people on ethnic lines. Some 30,000 troops secure the northern territory. From this position of strength, Denktash has been able to insist on terms for a confederal constitutional arrangement. Turkey is content, for the time being, to continue its occupation, judging that over time the division will come to be acknowledged, if not recognized, by the international community and the validity of the Greek-Cypriots' claim to represent the island as a whole will be eroded.

The Turkish-Cypriots insist that it is only Turkish troops, with their ethnic links, who are prepared to lay down their lives for them, and refuse to countenance any suggestion of a curb on a legal Turkish right of intervention in Cyprus. The idea that the proximity of Turkish forces on the mainland provides an adequate deterrent is dismissed as insufficient.

Furthermore, the Turkish-Cypriots have shown themselves prepared to enter into a federal arrangement only if they have full partnership status with legal safeguards to sustain it. The structure foreseen in the March 1986 Draft Framework Agreement, which was said to be the absolute limit of their concessions, would have so emasculated the power of action of the central government that there would have been even less likelihood of its successful operation than there was of the system which collapsed in the early 1960s. The presentation of the Turkish-Cypriot demands sometimes leaves the impression that they are designed with a view to creating such obstacles to negotiations that they will be certain to fail.

The Greek-Cypriots at first refused to accept the notion of a bizonal settlement believing that, as the division had been imposed by force of arms, they could persuade the international community to force Turkey to withdraw. This approach has failed, partly because of Turkey's adamantine resistance to such international censure as has been essayed, and partly because the Turkish-Cypriot community has become increasingly successful in obtaining a sympathetic hearing abroad for arguments that their security depends upon the rigorous separation of peoples.

Having finally accepted the concept of two provinces, the Greek-Cypriots have subsequently concentrated on the attainment of two main objectives: first to ensure their security by obtaining withdrawal of the Turkish troops and their replacement as guarantor forces (if guarantors are needed at all for an independent nation) by the troops of disinterested nations, and second to assure the basic human rights of freedom of movement, freedom of settlement, and freedom to own property.

The Greek-Cypriots have not, however, spoken with one voice in their approach to the problem, as the next Chapter will illustrate. They have divided into those who have accepted that the partition of the island is permanent and have sought to minimize the adverse consequences, and those who have been intent on reuniting the island with the Turkish-Cypriots as junior partners.

III. THE POLITICAL KALEIDOSCOPE

There is a tendency when discussing communal attitudes to the conflict to present them as though they were monolithic. In their broad concerns they are. The Greek-Cypriots seek to rid the country of the Turkish troops and settlers, to return the refugees to their homes and to reunite the Republic under a strong federal government. The Turkish-Cypriots want to sustain ethnic segregation and to pursue separate development under the security afforded by a Turkish troop presence.

The impression of single-mindedness has been reinforced by the fact that, until the election of Vassiliou in February 1988, each community had had only two leaders over the course of forty years and these were men who had been closely associated with the events leading to the division. Presidents Makarios and Kyprianou were both key figures in the struggle for *enosis*, while Dr Küçük and Mr Denktash were the principal exponents of *taksim*. All four brought a continuity of purpose to the problem and a rigidity of thought regarding the issues involved.

The Greek-Cypriots have a presidential system of government and strict separation of powers. The posts of member of the legislature and minister are incompatible. For the election of the House of Representatives a reinforced proportional representation system is used with three distributions of seats in the five electoral districts. The Turkish-Cypriots elect their president and members of parliament separately, but the government is drawn from the assembly in the Westminster manner. Voting for the legislature is by simple proportional representation.

Under the constitutions both of the Republic and of the TRNC, however, neither president is accountable to parliament. Thus, in uttering pronouncements or adopting negotiating positions, the community leaders have not had to reflect divergent points of view expressed within their respective legislatures.

There are, however, substantial differences of political opinion within each community. Each has four main parties and more than double that number of highly opinionated newspapers. There is strenuous debate over all aspects of public policy, including the national issue. For example, Greek-Cypriot communists seek demilitarization, while socialists and conservatives believe that the establishment of a countervailing Greek military presence would provide bargaining leverage. All Turkish-Cypriot parties say they feel a continued mainland military presence is necessary to guarantee security, though they are divided on the influence its presence gives Ankara in the running of their domestic politics.

Pre-1974
The growth of political parties was a late development. During colonial rule, the only representative institution was the municipal council[1] and, with the notable exception of the communists, members tended to have a local rather than an island-wide political focus. The

violence which preceded independence caused a majority to look to leaders focusing on ethnic rather than ideological issues. Dr Küçük was on the centre-right but his 'Cyprus is Turkish' Party was supported, initially at least, by separatists of all persuasions. Archbishop Makarios attracted support from across the political spectrum, his principal opposition coming from those who believed he was too politic in the prosecution of the *enosis* struggle.

The provision of separate voting in the 1960 constitution further emphasized this tendency. At independence, Makarios was elected president by the Greek-Cypriots,[2] and the Patriotic Front which supported him took 30 of the 35 Greek-Cypriot seats in the House of Representatives. The balance went to AKEL under the terms of a deal with the Archbishop whereby the party stood unopposed in five constituencies. Dr Küçük was elected vice president by the Turkish-Cypriots and his National Front Party took all 15 Turkish-Cypriot seats, while Denktash was elected chairman of the Turkish Communal Chamber.

The inter-communal fighting thrust militants to the fore. The Turkish-Cypriot leadership was dominated by separatists who suppressed those in their own community who promoted co-operation.[3] The Greek-Cypriot political leaders were men who had been prominent in EOKA. There were factions of various persuasions, each with its own militia, but they rallied round Archbishop Makarios and submerged their political differences for the sake of the inter-communal struggle.

Throughout the years of strife, the one significant political group which consistently abjured violence were the communists. Founded in 1926, the Cyprus Communist Party (*Kommounistikon Komma Kyprou* – KKK) was outlawed seven years later but re-emerged in 1941 as the Progressive Party of the Working People (AKEL). By the end of the decade it was the largest political organization on the island with significant representation at the municipal level.[4]

AKEL was proscribed by the British during the emergency (1955–9). From the underground, it agitated for self-determination but not for *enosis* and, as a consequence of what was perceived to be an anti-national attitude, came under attack from EOKA.[5] AKEL never built up a paramilitary force of its own for fear of providing a pretext for further reaction from nationalists.

At independence, Greece and Turkey proposed that the party should continue to be proscribed.[6] Makarios chose, however, to co-opt rather than to confront AKEL's political strength, though neither he nor any subsequent Greek-Cypriot leader has offered the party posts in government. The communists in turn supported Makarios' non-aligned policies and his opposition to partition which would have incorporated the island within NATO.

Party differentiation developed properly among the Greek-Cypriots only after 1968 when the unionist cause was set aside in favour of independence. Five parties emerged: the centre-right Unified Party under Glafkos Clerides; the conservative Progressive Front which incorporated the followers of former EOKA gunman Nikos Sampson; AKEL under Ezekias Papaioannou, its Secretary General since 1949; the Unified Democratic Social Union, a socialist party headed by Dr Vassos Lyssarides; and the pro-*enosis* Democratic National Party under Takis Evdokas. With the exception of AKEL, each party could count on the support of an unofficial militia.

Makarios remained a charismatic leader above parties. All pledged their support to him save the Democratic National Party which opposed his diversion from *enosis*. In the 1968 presidential elections Evdokas stood against Makarios but won a mere three per cent of the vote. In the 1970 elections for the House of Representatives, Clerides' conservatives topped the poll, though only because AKEL restricted the number of seats it contested.[7] Unionists gained no representation and took their campaign underground with the support of the Greek dictatorship. Makarios survived several assassination attempts and a complicated manoeuvre, orchestrated from Athens, to have the Church force his resignation. He was re-elected by acclamation in 1973 to the accompaniment of massive popular demonstrations.

Throughout this period, the Turkish-Cypriot leadership felt party politics to be a luxury their community could not afford. Indeed, the Basic Law made no provision for the establishment of parties as such. Members stood for the Communal Chamber as individuals representing interest groups. For the 1970 elections, Rauf Denktash formed the National Solidarity Front on the basis of a minimum programme designed to avoid internal divisions. It won handsomely, making Denktash the dominant figure on the Turkish-Cypriot scene, superseding Küçük. Left-wing opponents of Denktash used the law governing associations to form the Republican Turkish Party, but in the 1973 vice-presidential elections their candidate, Ahmet Berberoglu, was placed under house arrest and forbidden to participate on the grounds that the Turkish-Cypriots could not afford to be divided over national policy.[8]

Post-1974
THE GREEK-CYPRIOT POLITICAL SPECTRUM
Since 1974, four parties have dominated Greek-Cypriot political life:[9] the Democratic Rally (*Dimokratikos Synagermos* – DISY) which consolidated the conservative camp under Glafkos Clerides; AKEL which, until 1985, consistently had the largest voting strength at around 35 per cent; the Democratic Party (*Dimokratiko Komma* – DIKO), a centrist grouping headed by former foreign minister Spyros Kyprianou; and the Socialist Party (*Sosialistiko Komma, Ethniki Dimokratiki Enosi Kyprou* – EDEK)[10] which has drifted away from early third-world radicalism to a more social democratic posture along Scandinavian lines.

The consequences of the coup put paid to popular support for EOKA-B. Nikos Sampson was convicted of having unlawfully usurped the presidency and sentenced to 20 years' imprisonment, though he was released in April 1979 on health grounds.[11] Some others were pros-ecuted for specific crimes but, in the name of national unity, there was no general purge of EOKA-B supporters, even though remnants of the clandestine movement continued to perpetrate occasional terrorist acts as late as 1977. Despite such efforts to secure internal cohesion, however, the Greek-Cypriots split on their approach to the national issue and did so in such a way that the division assumed a political character.

DISY

Glafkos Clerides was retained by Makarios as inter-communal nego-tiator for more than a year after the Archbishop's return and resump-tion of the presidency, despite the fact that the two differed in their approach to the task. Clerides recognized early on that the Turkish side's minimum demand was a two-province federation and believed that the basic bargain would have to be a constitution which provided this in exchange for the withdrawal of Turkish troops. He argued that this should be done sooner rather than later in order to capitalize on international revulsion at the Turkish aggression. He judged that delay would dissipate this leverage and lead to the 'consolidation of a *fait accompli*'. Makarios, however, maintained a residual hope of reunification and nurtured the idea of administrative federation based on Turkish-Cypriot cantons. He believed that the Greek-Cypriots held the moral high ground and could afford 'a long struggle, if necessary' through the UN and other international fora. Early in 1976, Clerides was forced to resign both as negotiator and as president (speaker) of the House.

The centre-left parties aligned themselves with the president. They accused Clerides of being willing to accept partition to satisfy Western interests. In the October 1976 elections, AKEL, EDEK and Kyprianou's party, then known as the Democratic Front, formed an electoral pact to confront Clerides' DISY. The allies apportioned the seats between them – 21 to the Kyprianou group, nine to AKEL, four to EDEK and one to the independent Tassos Papadopoulos who had succeeded Clerides as negotiator. Although DISY polled a quarter of the vote it failed to take a single seat. Clerides had not helped himself by accepting into DISY some former members of EOKA-B, though he had done so on the grounds that it was better that they should have a place within the pol-itical system than be forced to operate without.

When Makarios died the following year, interim leadership fell to Kyprianou. He clearly did not provide the rallying focus that the Ethnarch had been, and Clerides set out to challenge him in the presi-dential election called for February 1978. He stood down, however, when a vestigial cell of EOKA-B kidnapped Kyprianou's son in a bid to secure the release of imprisoned fellows. In subsequent bids for the presidency in 1983 and 1988, Clerides was defeated as a consequence of AKEL throwing its vote behind centre-left candidates. The communists' alliance with DIKO in 1983 gave Kyprianou a first-round victory and, although in 1988 Clerides was the first-round front-runner, he was squeezed out by Vassiliou in the second round by 51.6 per cent to 48.4 per cent.

Clerides, the one senior political figure prepared to admit that Greek-Cypriots still 'dream' of union with Greece, has also been the most pragmatic about the concessions necessary to achieve a settlement – concessions which would ensure continued independence. He believes that the situation has become so ossified that there is no incentive for the Turkish troops to leave or for the Turkish-Cypriots to negotiate. He judges that if the situation remains unchanged for another decade the TRNC will acquire a degree of international recognition and all hope of federation will be lost. He would be prepared, therefore, to negotiate a compromise on the core Turkish-Cypriot demand regarding security and to permit, for a time, the continuation of a Turkish military presence. He would do this under the aegis of the Treaties of Guarantee and Alliance.

During the last presidential election campaign he proposed that at least 10,000 Greek troops should be brought to Cyprus as a counter-weight to the Turkish forces. He believes neither of the mainland nations is prepared to go to war over Cyprus and, therefore, that such a reinforcement would not present a danger while giving the Greek-Cypriots something with which to bargain. As part of a settlement, both sides would reduce their troop levels to a maximum of 5,000 men – fewer if possible – who would remain for a negotiated interim period to allow restoration of confidence. At the end of this period, numbers would be reduced over a further five years to the levels agreed in the original treaties. Clerides said NATO could monitor the process.

AKEL

DISY's willingness to see a continued presence on the island of troops from NATO nations has been fundamental to AKEL's opposition to Clerides. The communists' constant line has been that the July 1974 coup, organized by the pro-American Colonels in Athens, and the invasion, carried out by Turkey with US-supplied weaponry, were the culmination of Washington's efforts, begun a decade earlier through the Acheson plan, to partition Cyprus between the two NATO nations. As a counterbalance to what it perceives as America's determination to make Cyprus part of the West, AKEL has emphasized the need for a settlement to be found within a UN framework in which Eastern bloc views are also heard. It has argued that internal matters should be settled through inter-communal talks under UN auspices and external issues through an international conference at which, in addition to the two protagonists, permanent members of the UN Security Council plus some non-aligned nations would be represented. AKEL seeks an end to the tripartite Treaties of Alliance and Guarantee and their replacement by a UN guarantee. This would mean no further role for the UK in Cyprus affairs and, according to AKEL's reasoning, eliminate the justification for continuation of the SBAs, though the UK primarily views the bases from an international perspective and does not consider them directly pertinent to its role as a guarantor power.

Some Western analysts have perceived AKEL as a threat to Cypriot independence because of its pro-Moscow rhetoric which remained hardline long after Eurocommunism became fashionable among other West European parties. In large measure, though, this reflected the character of its leader, the dour, ex-Stalinist Ezekias Papaioannou, who was Secretary General for thirty-nine years until his death in 1988. His successor, Demetris Christofias, a man half his age, is expected to be more moderate, particularly in the light of the more liberal attitudes which now seem to prevail in the Kremlin.

In fact, it is largely through considerations of self-interest that AKEL has been a strong proponent of independence. Had *enosis* been achieved in the early years, the party would have been outlawed by the Greek authorities; equally, if the island were today an adjunct of Turkey, AKEL would be illegal under that country's anti-communism laws. AKEL recognizes that Cyprus is non-aligned within the Western sphere of influence. Thus, it has never bid for power in its own right or for direct participation in government. Instead, it has used its voting strength to broker governments which it feels will maintain an independent and non-aligned posture.

AKEL endorsed Makarios who reciprocated by allowing the party a place in the political life of the newly-formed country, despite the communists' failure to participate in the independence struggle. Its minimum programme of co-operation with Kyprianou was based on domestic considerations such as fiscal reform, expansion of education and the introduction of a health service. However, once he had used the agreement to outflank Clerides for the presidency, Kyprianou essentially ignored AKEL and, with urging from America and the UK, formally denounced the pact just prior to the 1985 New York summit.

Though opposing Clerides for president, AKEL was not beyond allying itself with DISY to retaliate against Kyprianou. Following the failure of the January 1985 summit, the two parties joined forces in the House of Representatives to censure Kyprianou for not accepting the Secretary General's proposed negotiating procedure. They sought to make it incumbent on the president to accept the will of the majority of the House which, not being required by the constitution, Kyprianou refused to do. The two parties engineered a dissolution of the legislature a year early, forcing new elections in December 1985 in which they sought the two-thirds majority necessary to amend the constitution. This collaboration proved too cynical even for the usually disciplined AKEL voters. As a result, the party's proportion of the vote dropped from 33 per cent to 27 per cent, while that of Kyprianou's DIKO rose from 19.5 per cent to 27.5 per cent. AKEL fell from first to third among the parties.

AKEL's support for the independent George Vassiliou in the 1988 presidential election ensured that Kyprianou would be unseated, though it also left open the possibility of a second-round win by the conservative Clerides. The party did not, therefore, press Vassiliou for left-wing policy concessions which might alienate centrist voters in the run-off against Clerides. AKEL was able to support Vassiliou because he did not represent one of the established parties and because his parents had been leading communist cadres in the late 1940s. He also had made some vague undertakings, such as the possibility of a referendum on whether to continue the Customs Union with the European Economic Community, which the communists oppose.

AKEL has always pursued co-operation with individual Turkish-Cypriots through its affiliated organizations, and its policy regarding a settlement would probably be even more accommodating did it not fear again being dubbed anti-national as it was in the 1950s.

DIKO

Spyros Kyprianou became involved in Cyprus politics while still a law student at Gray's Inn in England. In 1954, aged just 21, he was named the representative of the Ethnarchy in London and Washington. At independence, he became foreign minister, a post which he held for the next 12 years until Makarios succumbed to pressure from the dictatorship in Athens to replace him because of his recalcitrance in carrying out the wishes of the 'national centre'. Kyprianou remained out of politics for the next four years until his nomination as Makarios' effective heir.

In 1976 it was impossible to assess the true level of support for Kyprianou because of the electoral pact with AKEL and EDEK but, during the course of that parliament, 13 of the 21 deputies elected on his Democratic Front ticket defected to form three centrist parties. In the 1981 election Kyprianou's Democratic Party polled only 19.5 per cent and took just eight seats. Though DIKO became the second party after 1985, Kyprianou was never a president with a sound political power base. As a consequence, he was indecisive to the point of inaction. He brought to the job of president a precise, analytical mind and a fine capacity for subtle articulation but also a lack of imagination and a stubborn inflexibility.

Kyprianou pressed on with the inter-communal talks long after others believed the process to have been exhausted. He was determined that any settlement should create a united country and not some form of sovereignty association with restrictions on movement and continued segregation. The Turkish-Cypriot declaration of independence only served to make his stance more rigid. He saw it as reflecting the 'law of the jungle' – might is right – and it deeply affronted his legal sensibility. He reacted with a sense of injury and moral indignation whenever the international community appeared to be asking him to agree to any concession without first insisting upon withdrawal of Turkish troops. Ultimately, this clouded his capacity even to give the appearance of willingness to compromise, particularly over the UN Secretary General's proposed Draft Agreements. This damaged Cyprus' diplomatic advantage, and in the last two years of his presidency Kyprianou became increasingly defensive and ineffectual.

In 1986, he introduced a levy[12] on earnings to help finance a $250-million programme to re-equip the National Guard with modern tanks, personnel carriers, helicopters, anti-armour rockets and surface-to-air missiles (SAM). Kyprianou offered to dismantle the Guard and cancel outstanding equipment orders if the Turkish forces and settlers would leave the island. He proposed that internal and external security should be provided by an international UN peace force of up to 30,000 men whose composition and terms of reference would be provided by the Security Council. Greece and the Cyprus government undertook to underwrite a substantial part of the cost.[13] The suggestion was rejected by the Turkish-Cypriots who said that UNFICYP, which is only mandated to use arms in self-defence, had not been able to protect them from Greek-Cypriot attacks. Only Turkish troops were prepeared to shed blood in their defence. The Turkish General Staff responded to the Greek-Cypriot arms refurbishment by increasing the Turkish troop strength on the island by nearly one third to over 30,000 and modernizing its armour.

Kyprianou had an equivocal relationship with Athens. Because of his feud with the Colonels he resented any implication of operating under instruction, yet he consulted with the Greek leadership more frequently than might be deemed seemly for the leader of an independent nation. He angered the conservative New Democracy government when he dismissed out of hand the 1978 US-UK-Canadian plan with its proposals for power-sharing in exchange for significant territorial concessions and troop withdrawals by Turkey.[14] Papandreou's line that Cyprus was an issue of occupation and invasion which ought to be resolved in the international arena was consistent with Kyprianou's own thinking and made it easier for him to be less accommodating towards Denktash and his demands for equal status at the inter-communal bargaining table. Yet Kyprianou's pact with AKEL infuriated the Greek leader who, despite his radical reputation, is decidedly anti-communist. Papandreou's policy statement on the eve of the 1985 legislative assembly elections in Cyprus, insisting on Turkish troop withdrawals prior to a settlement, was obviously designed to shore up Kyprianou's hard line.[15] But Papandreou's meeting with Ozal at Davos, with its inception of a process of *rapprochement* with Ankara, coming just two weeks before the 1988 presidential elections, undermined Kyprianou's last defence of his unyielding posture.

EDEK

The Socialist Party has influence which far outstrips its voting strength. The party's appeal is to urban intellectuals, and it was active in the resistance against the Colonels, forging close links with Papandreou's Panhellenic Liberation Movement. EDEK maintained one of the most active militias[16] which, for a time, before the creation of the tactical police reserve, was the only military force loyal to Makarios confronting unionist terrorists. Its members were particular targets during the coup and many of its leaders were killed.

The head of the party, Vassos Lyssarides, believes that the Western powers are not unhappy with the present state of affairs in Cyprus, a stasis which passes for stability. He argues that to break the stalemate requires confrontation. In the 1985 elections he argued, like Clerides, for the despatch of a large Greek military contingent to Cyprus, although his assumption was that Turkey would regard this as a *casus belli* which would create a crisis that would force Cyprus back onto the US and NATO foreign-policy agenda and hopefully provoke a settlement. He has supported re-equipment of the armed forces to provide sufficient defensive capability to hold off a Turkish advance until such time as the international community could intervene.

Lyssarides was elected president of the House of Representatives following the 1985 elections and, together with Kyprianou, Papandreou and Archbishop Chrysostomos, leader of the Orthodox Church, formed an unofficial rejectionist front opposing all calls for further Greek-Cypriot compromise. The quarrel, he argued, was with Ankara, not with the Turkish-Cypriots, and no concessions could be made which would allow Turkey any benefit from its invasion and occupation of a once-sovereign state.

Vassiliou

The election of the independent George Vassiliou as president of the Republic of Cyprus in February 1988 represented a rejection of such unproductive negativity and a wish to begin again to explore the prospects for reunification. Vassiliou's attitude is that a settlement is desirable – though not at any price. Everything is negotiable, but concessions to the Turkish-Cypriots will have to be matched by flexibility on their part towards Greek-Cypriot sensitivities.

Vassiliou is something of a political enigma. He is the son of parents with a deep intellectual commitment to communism. His father, a doctor, travelled to Greece to serve with the communist Democratic Army at a time when it had already become obvious that it was doomed to defeat. He went into exile in the Soviet Union where, after initial privations, he was allowed to return to the practice of medicine, becoming relatively well-off. The young Vassiliou began his studies in Hungary but fled West during the uprising in 1956 and continued at the London School of Economics. The family returned to Cyprus after independence.

George Vassiliou established a market research firm which does consultancy work throughout the Middle East. The firm flourished on the back of the two Arab oil embargoes, making Vassiliou sufficiently wealthy to indulge his intellectual pursuit of politics as an independent. He has no party machine but has come to power with the tacit support of AKEL. His personal politics, however, appear to be liberal rather than left-wing. He endorses the Gorbachev reforms of communism and the consequent improvement in East–West relations. Like most Cypriots, he subscribes to the thesis that the US does not press Ankara to quit Cyprus because of its concern to sustain Turkey as a bulwark against Soviet penetration in the Middle East. That said, he understands better than many of his countrymen that US leverage in Ankara is limited. Vassiliou believes that the global relaxation of tension and the general disengagement process heralded by developments in Afghanistan, southern Africa and Central America could increasingly provide an appropriate climate for a Cyprus settlement. Although Cyprus is in no way a direct counter in any East–West bargaining, he believes that the general reduction in tension could make the US more inclined to try to persuade Turkey to be more amenable.

Vassiliou has resurrected the National Council of party leaders to advise the president and has consulted regularly with them. However, he is a firm believer in strong leadership and insists that it is he who will take the final decisions. His style of government is more that of the corporate boardroom than of the traditional political cabinet. He gives an initial impression of having no particular taste for power for its own sake and therefore a willingness to stand answerable for any settlement concessions. He has said that he will put any settlement to a referendum.

Politics within the Turkish-Cypriot community

At the inception of the Turkish Federated State of Cyprus in 1975, Denktash was named president. Initially, he established himself as a political president at the head of the conservative National Unity Party (*Ulusal Birlik Partisi* – UBP). After the creation of the Turkish Republic of Northern Cyprus (TRNC) in 1983, he declared himself to be above party politics, though he has remained clearly identified with conservative elements who favour intimate ties with Turkey. Latterly he has come to see himself as the 'founding father' of the TRNC, and his rhetoric has drawn increasingly on his own precepts as the basic tenets for the conduct of public life. His administration is replete with sycophantic placemen to such an extent that the opposition parties allege that the TRNC is evolving into a one-party state.[17]

In a perverse way, the arrival of the Turkish troops can be said to have been responsible for the introduction of party politics among the Turkish-Cypriots. The security they afforded meant that at last internal differences could be freely expressed. Parties began to form within the Constitutent Assembly called to create the charter for the TFSC. The political community is exceedingly factious, and at one point there were 12 parties simultaneously in operation.[18] Three, however, have predominated: the UBP which favours close association with Turkey, the centre-left Communal Liberation Party (*Toplumcu Kurtuluş Partisi* – TKP) which split over the issue of independence, and the left-wing Republican Turkish Party (*Cumhuriyetçi Türk Partisi* – CTP) which favours greater inter-communal contacts to promote an early federal settlement. There also has been a succession of groups representing the interests of settlers, the latest being the New Birth Party (*Yeni Doğus Partisi* – YDP).[19]

The multiplicity of parties is a reaction to the years before 1974 when particular interests were subordinated to the common cause. Practically, however, the situation has remained the same, with the UBP in power since separation – either in its own right or in coalitions made with minority parties or splinter groups from major parties. As a consequence there has been no serious political challenge to Denktash's presentation of the Turkish-Cypriot case. That said, all parties fundamentally agree on basic national issues such as the maintenance of ethnic homogeneity and a Turkish military guarantee for the northern province. It is over matters such as the role of the settlers and the pace and forms of *rapprochement* that they differ. Domestic political differences have focused on the economy.

UBP

Denktash won the first presidential elections in 1976, with a substantial 77.6 per cent of the vote. The CTP candidate, Ahmet Berberoglu, was permitted to run on this occasion but the electorate obviously saw Denktash as a symbol of continuity around whom it could rally. The opposition took some consolation from the fact that 30 per cent of voters did not turn out. The UBP took 30 of the 40 seats in the elections to the House of Representatives which took place on the same day. In the course of the government's five-year term, however, it was riven by factionalism. There were three Prime Ministers, the first of whom, Neçat Konuk, broke away to form his own Democratic People's Party.

By the time of the June 1981 elections, people felt more secure and were ready to express opinions about the day-to-day running of public life. Denktash was re-elected, from a field of five presidential candidates, but only with a scant 51.8 per cent majority vote. In the House, the UBP obtained just 18 of the 40 seats. The TKP[20] took 13 and the CTP six, but efforts by the two to form a coalition with the Democratic People's Party were frustrated, it has been alleged, by the military regime then ruling in Ankara.[21] A minority UBP government took office but was brought down before the end of the year over its economic programme. In February 1982, it was reinstated in coalition with minority parties, one of which was the Turkish Unity Party representing settlers' interests. The opposition parties identify this as the turning point since which there has been no real opportunity to advance an alternative to the obdurate conservative viewpoint on the national issue.[22]

Denktash's decision to declare independence was supported by the UBP and the settlers' parties but opposed by the left-wing Republican Turkish Party. The Communal Liberation Party split on the issue but, when the vote was taken on 15 November 1983, there were still enough TKP members who opposed the unilateral declaration of independence that, together with the CTP, they could have prevented the two-thirds majority necessary for passage. Just days before the vote was taken, however, the government introduced emergency measures legislation which provided powers similar to those prevailing under martial law in Turkey and, on the eve of the declaration, Denktash convened members of the assembly to tell them that any party or individual who voted against independence would be banned in the new republic. When the vote was taken the outcome was unanimous.

Within days, the House voted again to refashion itself as an enlarged Constituent Assembly for the purpose of creating a new constitution. This time the majority was 26–14, which opponents of UDI argue would have been the outcome of the independence poll had it not been conducted under duress. The Constituent Assembly was to consist of the 40 existing members of the House of Representatives plus a further 30 nominees. Ten of the nominations were in the gift of Denktash and five were to be former members of TMT. Left-wing representatives were excluded.[23] The size of the House of Representatives foreseen under the new constitution was increased to 50 but the role of the executive was strengthened at the expense of the legislature.

A referendum on the constitution was postponed pending the outcome of the series of UN peace initiatives which culminated in the abortive January 1985 New York summit. When the vote was finally taken in March 1985, the result was 69 per cent in favour, although there was a high abstention rate and, overall, only 54 per cent of the electorate voted 'yes'. The opposition parties claim that the decisive votes were cast by settlers, and that had the poll been solely based on Turkish-Cypriot votes the constitution would not have been approved.

One of the effects of the new constitution was that Denktash, who under the previous charter would have had to stand down after his second term, was able to run again. He won the June 1985 presidential contest decisively, taking 70 per cent of the popular vote. The National Unity Party, however, took only 24 seats in the newly enlarged House. The UBP leader, Derviş Eroğlu, entered into talks to form a coalition with the New Birth Party (YDP) but these foundered on the settlers' party's demands that all four of its House members should be given cabinet posts. A tenuous coalition was formed with the Communal Liberation Party but eventually broke up over economic policy. The YDP then agreed to join the government with just one cabinet post for its leader, Aytaç Beşeşler, a retired Turkish officer who settled in Cyprus in 1976. This arrangement collapsed after Beşeşler lost the

YDP leadership but was reconstituted in May 1988 when he returned to government as an independent. Eroğlu is on record as saying that 'the Turkish-Cypriot people constitute an inalienable part of the Turkish nation'.[24] In announcing the 1988 cabinet he pledged his government 'to promote integration with Turkey.'[25]

Partly because of the perpetual political manoeuvring and partly because of the overweening personality of Denktash, it has been difficult to view UBP policy as anything other than his. Denktash refutes suggestions that he is a cat's-paw for Ankara. Rather his identification with Turkey is absolute and he believes that this should be the case for the Turkish-Cypriot community as a whole. A typical exhortation is '. . . We smile when the motherland smiles; we soar when the motherland soars; and we exist so long as the motherland exists'.[26] Such an attitude allows him to accept with relatively good grace changes in mainland policy which would leave a lesser devotee disgruntled. For example, he was known not to be happy with what he considered to be concessions contained in the March 1986 Draft Framework Agreement but, having been advised by Ankara to accept it, did so and stuck doggedly by the document as his minimum negotiating position for the next two years. When advised not to insist on it as a precondition to talks with Vassiliou, he shelved the Agreement with almost the same alacrity as he had taken it on board.

TKP
The Communal Liberation Party does not differ from the ruling group on matters of substance regarding a solution to the Cyprus problem, though it does approach matters from a different perspective. The split over UDI prompted a number of bitterly contested leadership battles. The current head is Mustafa Akinçi, mayor of Turkish-Cypriot Nicosia for the past decade. He supported independence on the grounds that it would give equality at the bargaining table and help the Turkish-Cypriots to emerge from the tutelage of the mainland government.

Under his leadership, TKP's policy is that segregation should not be permanent but that amalgamation must, of necessity, be very gradual. The best guarantee will be the establishment of trust, and to this end the party urges contacts on specific, practical matters. For example, it has suggested the creation of a federal co-ordination council to discuss harmonization of taxation and joint investment programmes. As mayor, Akinçi has co-operated in the construction of a joint sewage system for the capital and in a UN master-plan co-ordinating the roads, housing and industrial development towards the day of possible reunification.

Akinçi believes that the boundary between the provinces should be open and that there must be freedom of movement for both communities from the outset of a settlement in order to symbolize the unity of the federation. The rights of ownership of property and freedom of settlement cannot be rejected in principle but must be implemented in such a way that bizonal federation is ensured. He suggests the best way to achieve this would be a property-swap, and compensation for refugees on both sides. He calls for a mutual reduction of forces to levels where neither side feels threatened by the other – possibly 5,000–7,000 men on either side. The party wants Turkey to retain a military guarantee but says that the responsibility for invoking it should reside with the Turkish-Cypriot legislature and not with Ankara.

The TKP does not support the expulsion of settlers who arrived in the immediate aftermath of 1974, arguing that this would simply create a new refugee problem. But it does firmly oppose policies fostering fresh immigration, such as legislation permitting Turkish investors to import their workforce from the mainland, a practice which the party says exacerbates the settler problem, denies jobs to locals and depresses wages. It has vigorously opposed the creation of the settler parties, arguing that a party ought to represent a political philosophy and not just narrow sectional interests related to the area of origin of its constituency.

The TKP challenges the UBP assertion that the economic problems of the north are simply the result of the Greek-Cypriot economic embargo and calls for a greater degree of public sector development of local industry and an end to the government's preferential treatment of mainland Turkish investors. It seeks monetary reform to curb the soaring inflation imported through the use of the Turkish lira.

CTP

The Republican Turkish Party (CTP) headed by Özker Özgür is decried by the UBP as a Marxist organization in league with AKEL. Özgür insists that the party believes in pluralism and is not communist but 'progressive socialist'. The Marxist label stuck after CTP and TKP representatives met and issued a joint statement with members of AKEL and DIKO during the World Peace Council meeting in Sofia in 1980, a meeting which Denktash made much of during the bitterly contested 1981 election campaign.[27]

Özgür is of two minds about whether the party should have accepted the ultimatum to vote for independence. The caucus decided that, on balance, it was better to remain active in order to be able to continue to campaign for reunification rather than be consigned to the sidelines. CTP is overtly federalist[28] but believes the process of reintegration will be a long-term process. In principle, Özgür accepts the three freedoms for citizens of both communities but is prepared to accept temporary restrictions until a climate of confidence has been created.

Özgür believes that the mainland troops are perceived by a majority of Turkish-Cypriots as being vital to their survival, and would be prepared to see a symbolic presence remain as part of a guarantee process. The balance should withdraw according to a clearly defined timetable, but *after*, not before, a settlement has been agreed between the north and south of the island. Both Turkey and Greece would need to be involved in the guarantee arrangements, but the UK should be

45

replaced, perhaps by members of the UN Security Council adopting joint responsibility. The CTP believes that the SBAs are incompatible with the non-aligned status of Cyprus and should be dismantled.

The party expresses particular concern about the settlers. Özgür agrees with the Greek-Cypriot estimate of their number and says more continue to come. He claims that they have been allocated housing and land at the expense of indigenous Turkish-Cypriots and, more importantly, have disrupted the balance of power within the Turkish-Cypriot community by reinforcing separatist tendencies. CTP believes that the settlers should be compensated and returned to the mainland.

YDP
The parties representing the settlers have been fissiparous. Beşeşler, interviewed at a time when he still headed the YDP, said it was common in every nation that after a period of years immigrants became involved in the political process. So long as Denktash was felt to be doing a good job, the settlers would continue to support him. Beşeşler believed Cyprus had a 'special relationship' with Turkey but supported an independent federal state.

The influence of politics on prospects for a settlement
The fundamental differences between Makarios and Clerides concerned their approach to the solution but they also reflected an element of political rivalry. When Clerides succeeded Sampson in July 1974, he assumed the title of president and not of acting president as, constitutionally, he might have been expected to do. He governed briefly with the cabinet which had been appointed under Sampson, which his opponents say tarnished his democratic credentials, and he advised against the early return of Makarios. He implied that the Archbishop's presence would re-open divisions in Greek-Cypriot ranks and hamper a solution. His detractors argued that he sought to keep Makarios away for his own political benefit. Once Makarios did come back, on 7 December 1974, the two men resumed co-operation for the sake of the larger national cause but, ultimately, Makarios was party to the manoeuvring which forced Clerides to stand down as inter-communal negotiator in April 1976 and as president of the Assembly later that summer. Nor did the Archbishop prevent the formation of the electoral alliance which in the October 1976 parliamentary election froze out Clerides and DISY from the House of Representatives.

It was paradoxical that Clerides, who represented the right, the traditional proponents of *enosis*, found himself arguing the case for an accommodation with Turkey in opposition to the centre and left which, prior to the coup and invasion, had espoused inter-communal talks and continued independence. The many ambiguities inherent in this situation hampered Greek-Cypriot efforts to arrive at a common negotiating posture at an early stage when the Turkish-Cypriots had not yet consolidated their institutions in the north and when Turkey might have been more susceptible to international pressure to accept a settlement.

So long as the Archbishop was alive there was little likelihood of Clerides becoming president. After the Archbishop's death, however, Clerides became a prime contender, though he did not command sufficient support to win over other candidates if they had the backing of AKEL. Kyprianou inherited the mantle of leadership from Makarios but never had a major power base in his own right. However, by adopting the Archbishop's policy of 'a long struggle, if necessary' he was able to appeal to the significant refugee constituency, and this factor, coupled with AKEL's fears of Clerides' residual sympathy for *enosis* caused the communists to throw their weight behind Kyprianou for a period of years.

Over the course of years, AKEL evolved an increasingly federative stance, yet nonetheless found it expedient to make common cause with Kyprianou because of its overriding concern that a deal struck under Clerides might mean an end to the country's non-aligned status. After Kyprianou's abrupt renunciation of his minimum programme with AKEL in December 1984, the communists felt free to press openly for federation and even to co-operate with Clerides in seeking to get rid of Kyprianou. But they were not prepared to support the conservative leader in office and instead afforded their substantial support to the independent Vassiliou.

Without conceding any authority as president of the Republic, Vassiliou has gone further towards meeting Denktash in the latter's capacity as a communal leader than either of his predecessors were prepared to go. This has been possible partly because he has no party to satisfy and partly because it has become increasingly clear to Greek-Cypriots across the political spectrum that, if they do not achieve a settlement in the relatively near future, the division of the island will become permanent. As a consequence, there has been less domestic political criticism of Vassiliou for having adopted a more accommodating attitude than might have been expected. At the same time, his resurrection of the National Council has allowed for a more discreet airing of policy differences. Vassiliou continues to have the tacit support of AKEL and, because of his willingness to negotiate, the co-operation of Clerides, at least for the time being. Vassiliou is said to respect Clerides' considerable knowledge of the Turkish-Cypriots arising from his many years of involvement in the inter-communal talks. Lyssarides, though still fundamentally opposed to concessions to the Turkish-Cypriots, gives the appearance of having mellowed in his capacity as the Speaker of the Assembly in which capacity he is acting President. He comports himself with greater gravity and increasingly casts himself in the mould of intellectual elder statesman. Kyprianou, still bruised by his electoral defeat, continues to bridle at the idea of treating with the Turkish-Cypriots while the Turkish troops remain and, for the moment, remains odd man out.

For all the politicking on the Turkish-Cypriot side there is greater unity of purpose on the national question than among the Greek-Cypriots. Denktash still defines the fundamental aspirations of the smaller community for security and autonomy. All the parties accept that the Turkish troops have prevented them from being subsumed as a minority and believe that a residual mainland force will be necessary, for a time at least, in order to ensure their interests in any federal structure. Equally, all the parties feel there must be continued residential separation of peoples, probably until after the passing of the three generations of people who have experienced the bitter divisions first of the communities and then of the island.

The principal differences between the Turkish-Cypriot parties lie in their attitudes towards the mainland. Denktash and many of his associates have a greater affinity with Turkey than with Cyprus; they conceive of themselves primarily as Turks and not as Cypriots and are prepared to pursue policies which make the TRNC more an outpost of Ankara than an adjunct of a federated republic. Parties representing settlers' interests have inclined to a similar view and between them they have managed, with Turkish assistance, to maintain a hold on government. Not all those who vote for Denktash subscribe to such attitudes but nonetheless they continue to support him in office because the forcefulness of his personality sustains the TRNC and thus their autonomy. The opposition parties are more inclined to a Cypriot perspective and believe that re-integration with the south could be more advantageous than forever being dragged along on the periphery of Turkey's seemingly perpetual political and economic instability. But they too prefer Turkish to Greek-Cypriot tutelage and are only prepared to reunite on terms which guarantee their rights as a separate community.

The opposition parties' principal differences with Denktash are over economic policy. Both the TKP and the CTP believe that there are advantages to be gained through a settlement which would end international isolation and allow integration with the dynamic economy of the south. In their view such a development would preclude what they see as increasing economic colonization by Turkey, with all that entails in terms of inflation and indebtedness.

IV. ECONOMIC CONSIDERATIONS

The disparity in economic development between the two sectors of the island is substantial and accelerating. *Per capita* income in the south is approaching $US 7,000 a year which exceeds the levels on the Greek and Turkish mainlands. By comparison, official Turkish-Cypriot *per capita* income stands at just a quarter of that sum.

Greek-Cypriot recovery
The Turkish invasion caused enormous dislocation. The territory seized contained approximately 80 per cent of the citrus groves, 65 per cent of the wheat-fields, 45 per cent of industry and 67 per cent of tourist installations. Losses in materials, equipment, consumer goods and cash ran into billions of dollars.[1] The principal port of Famagusta was captured along with its tourist suburb of Varosha, though the latter with its 'riviera' complex of hotels has been sealed off and left unoccupied. Nicosia international airport was bombed and remains out of commission. It now lies within the buffer zone and forms part of UNFICYP headquarters. Both Varosha and the airport have featured prominently as bargaining counters in the prolonged negotiations.

The Greek-Cypriot government decided that refugees displaced from the north should not be consigned to the sort of ghettoes created, for example, by the Palestinians in the Middle East. An estimated $600 m was invested, most of it before 1980, in the construction of housing estates and related services in major urban centres and in the refurbishment of abandoned Turkish-Cypriot properties as temporary accommodation. More than half the funding was provided by the state, although 18 per cent of its contribution has come from aid from foreign agencies and governments. Industrial estates were established in Nicosia, Larnaca, Limassol and Paphos to provide jobs for the refugees.[2]

Priority was given to investments with export potential both in light and medium industry and in agriculture. Private entrepreneurs erected new hotels all along the south coast and, despite limited numbers of arrivals in the immediate aftermath of the fighting, tourism has been one of the prime factors in the south's recovery. The emergency development programme achieved double figure GDP growth in the early years, though this slowed markedly by the end of the decade and in the 1980s it has ranged between 3 and 8.8 per cent.

Cyprus has the third highest number of university graduates *per capita* in the world after the US and Canada, and investors have gradually been reorienting towards higher technology. Agriculture, which provided 37 per cent of GDP before the Turkish invasion, comprised just 7.3 per cent in 1987, with manufacturing accounting for 16.4 per cent.[3] The government has promoted Cyprus as an offshore financial services centre and the country has benefitted enormously from the upheaval in the Lebanon. A total of 4,757 offshore companies had registered at the end of 1987 and some 700 of them maintained fully-staffed offices. Several insurance and banking corporations have established regional headquarters in Greek-Cypriot Nicosia and banking, insurance and real estate contributed 16.8 per cent of GDP in 1987.

The deficit financing necessary to achieve such redevelopment has left the south with an external debt estimated by the State Planning Office in 1987 to be $1.4 bn or 38 per cent of GDP. Nearly 40 per cent of that is attributable to the public sector which in 1987 continued to run a budget deficit totalling 4.4 per cent of GDP.

The persistent trade deficit totalled $762 m in 1987, but that year, for the first time in two decades, the current account was in the black, $97 m in surplus. Provisional figures for 1988 suggest another surplus, although of a lesser magnitude.

Turkish-Cypriot stagnation

By comparison, the economy of the northern territory has remained in the doldrums. The Turkish-Cypriots argue that there was a concerted effort by the Greek-Cypriots during the mid-1960s to 'drive them out of the economy' through the blockade of the enclaves. According to the TRNC State Planning Organization, the Turkish-Cypriot contribution to the GDP of Cyprus declined from 17.9 per cent in 1963 to a mere 5.1 per cent in 1964. During the next decade its average annual contribution was just 6 per cent.[4]

Virtually no statistics were kept in the north between 1974 and 1977, but heavy injections of Turkish aid are believed to have ensured a high rate of growth in the early years. The main thrust of activity was the rehabilitation of refugees. However, resettlement was effected largely by the allocation of abandoned Greek-Cypriot properties; a concerted public housing programme did not begin until the early 1980s, and then it was plagued by financing problems. Sanayii Holding, a state enterprise, took over the operation of some abandoned industrial premises but many others were left to moulder. As late as 1986, 31.4 per cent of the population worked on the land contributing just 12.5 per cent of GDP, while only 8.5 per cent were employed in manufacturing contributing 8.9 per cent.[5] The state was the largest employer with 22.9 per cent of the economically active population on the payroll. The State Planning Organization blames lack of domestic resources and inadequate aid, and says that in the circumstances 'the realisation of 3 per cent rate of growth should be assessed as a significant achievement'.[6] The Central Bank reported an increase of 7.8 per cent in 1985 and 4.7 per cent in 1986 but, as this was from a low base, it has not narrowed the gap vis-à-vis the south. Smuggling with the mainland (and with the south) has been rife, and Central Bank officials privately acknowledge that the black economy is such that real per capita income is probably twice the figure suggested by official statistics.

The introduction of the Turkish Lira (TL) as legal tender brought with it currency instability and imported inflation. For a time it was artificially pegged against the dollar but, once allowed to float, it plummetted to a small fraction of its original value.[7] The official rate of inflation peaked at 124 per cent in 1979. Austerity measures had reduced this to an official figure of 43 per cent by 1987, although businessmen claim the real rate was half as high again. Bank lending rates in 1988 stood at 68 per cent.

The territory has run a persistent trade deficit which climbed from $50 m in 1980 to $152 m in 1987, though the current account deficit has been kept in check by rapidly expanding tourist revenues which have increased from $24 m to $88.5 m over the same period. The number of tourists nearly trebled over the period and was estimated to have reached 200,000 in 1988. Initially, because of the Greek-Cypriot transport embargo, virtually all tourists came from the Turkish mainland, but in 1988 nearly a quarter came from other countries. The authorities see tourism as a motor for the economy and have embarked upon a major programme of subsidies and cheap credit for tourist operations. North Cyprus Turkish Airlines, which previously operated with planes leased from Turkish Airways, has decided to purchase its own aircraft.

Budget revenues have consistently met less than half of the administration's outgoings. The budget approved for 1988 totalled TL 171.2 bn ($138.5 m at current exchange rates) of which just over 45 per cent was to be met from local resources. Turkey was to provide TL 57 bn ($46 m) in aid and TL 36.9 bn ($29.9 m) in credits. The high public sector wage bill consumes more than a third of the budget, leaving little for development investment. Infrastructure spending has largely been financed by foreign borrowing, mainly from the Agricultural Bank of Turkey. In 1986 the accumulated debt stood at TL 45.9 bn ($68 m),[8] a modest 24 per cent of GDP, but this does not take into account the direct grant aid from Turkey. Ankara has agreed a moratorium on repayment of this assistance and the TRNC Central Bank hopes it may eventually be written off.

In 1986, the Eroğlu government signed a protocol with Ankara designed to introduce the sorts of free market reforms being implemented by the Ozal government on the mainland. It provided for freer trade with Turkey, incentives for investment particularly by foreigners, closure of uneconomic State Economic Enterprises, reduction of the civil service complement by 15 per cent and more rigorous domestic revenue collection. The opposition claimed that this paved the way for exploitation of Turkish-Cypriots by mainland businessmen, and the decision to go ahead with the agreement led to the break up of the coalition with the Communal Liberation Party. The administration argues that it will encourage Turkish-Cypriot enterprise by reducing the inefficient state sector. It is as yet too early to assess the overall effects of these reforms.

Infrastructure

The division of the island has led to a duplication of facilities. Loss of the international airport severely disrupted communications with the island. In the south, a new international airport was opened at Larnaca as early as February 1975. A smaller field for tourist traffic was opened at Paphos in 1983. Turkey claims that the latter, hidden behind the Troodos mountain range, could be used to land Greek troops from the mainland in the event of renewed hostilities.

In the north, it was not until July 1977 that the former light aircraft strip at Tymbou, near Nicosia, was upgraded to international standard and renamed Erçan. A second airfield large enough to take wide-bodied jets or heavy military transports has been constructed at Geçitkale (formerly Lefkoniko), inland from Famagusta. It is said to be equipped with the latest automatic instrument landing devices but has no proper terminal. The field, inaugurated in 1986, was used for commercial traffic during an extension to Erçan but then mothballed. It is believed to be intended for military purposes although Turkish officials insist it merely constitutes an alternative emergency landing strip in order to comply with international air transport regulations. In the event of a settlement involving Turkish troop withdrawals, Geçitkale would facilitate a rapid reintroduction of forces, provided it remained under Turkish-Cypriot control.

Until 1974, Famagusta was the island's principal port, but after it fell to the Turks the Greek-Cypriot authorities undertook substantial works to modernize Limassol and Larnaca and a new bulk terminal was constructed at Vasilikos to service the cement and mining industries. Limassol now accounts for nearly half of all the cargo handled on the island.

In the north both merchant ships and the Turkish navy use Famagusta where a free port zone was established in 1983. An alternative ferry port was completed at Kyrenia in 1987 with a draught sufficient to accommodate Turkey's new *Yavuz*-class frigates. Troop reinforcements could be landed there by high-speed hydrofoil from Tasuou or Mersin in approximately two hours.

The principal electricity generating installations are in the south. The Electricity Authority of Cyprus will have 504 MW of oil-fired capacity installed by 1989, but such is the rate of growth of the economy that it plans to augment this with a further 720 MW of coal-burning plant in the next 10–15 years. The Turkish military brought 50 MW of emergency generating capacity to the island and this has been connected to the grid to help meet peak summer demands. The Electricity Authority continues to provide power to the north without receiving payment. The accumulated loss of revenue in 1987 was estimated to have reached $200 m.[9] The Turkish-Cypriot authorities argue that this in part compensates for what they consider to have been inequitable Greek-Cypriot distribution of international aid.[10] Greek-Cypriot hardliners have proposed that the power should be cut but moderates fear that this could provide a cause for further Turkish action. Moreover, they argue it is inconsistent with the concept of seeking to reunite the peoples of the island. In summer 1987, there were a series of cuts and 'brown-outs' in the north. The Turkish-Cypriot press alleged that these had been engineered purposely by the south to disrupt Turkish-Cypriot tourist traffic, but the Electricity Authority insisted that the system simply could not cope with demand. Turkish authorities are considering supplying the TRNC with power from the mainland by sub-sea cable.

The south has continued to provide power because it gets water from the north. About 30 per cent of the island's supplies arise in the TRNC. The south has embarked upon a $270 m scheme, known as the Southern Conveyer Project, to transport water from the Troodos mountains to the tourist resorts and farms along the southern coast. A proposal to provide fresh water to the north by pipeline from Turkey was deemed to be too expensive and a new system of dams and reservoirs is, therefore, being constructed.

Re-establishing the balance
It is widely held in both communities that a programme to end the economic imbalance must be a major feature of any settlement package. The United States has pledged $250 m in aid in the event that there is 'significant progress'. The European Community has promised soft loans and grants under a Third Financial Protocol agreed in conjunction with the 1987 Customs Union agreement. The sums remain to be negotiated.[11] In 1985, the Reagan Administration offered $1 bn towards the creation of a central Purchasing Fund which would act as a land bank, buying Greek property in Turkish areas at full market value and selling it cheaply to Turkish-Cypriots and *vice versa*. This is a potentially very constructive and practical measure since many refugees will not wish to live among the other community but, equally, it is politically sensitive because the presupposition that many refugees will not want to return to their homes runs counter to official Greek-Cypriot policy. In the south, Turkish-Cypriot properties that have been allocated to refugees are managed by an administrative committee which holds title deeds and collects rents which are paid into a special state fund. The constitution of the TRNC, however, precludes the return to Greek-Cypriots of their former properties in the north. It asserts that all abandoned landholdings and dwellings have become the property of the new state. The administration has issued certificates of usufruct to their present Turkish-Cypriot inhabitants though they are ambiguously entitled Final Use Certificates. The constitution says laws will be introduced governing compensation.

During the 1988–9 round of talks, Denktash is reported to have said that the right of free movement would only be restored after all property claims had been settled, in order to avoid conflicts over ownership. Thereafter, he is reported to have said that the Greek-Cypriots would have a right of establishment in the TRNC – not a right of resettlement – but only after a period of years. Eighteen years has been suggested, though just why this particular figure was proposed was not immediately apparent. Purchases of land in the north by Greek-Cypriots would be regulated by municipal authorities so that the Turkish-Cypriot population would not be diluted.

The Greek-Cypriots have not indicated what their response would be to such a scheme though they can be expected at least initially to oppose it. They must, however, exercise nice judgement in the matter since there are those in the Turkish-Cypriot administration who argue that there is no need for property settlements because there were none following the mass population exchanges between mainland Greece and Turkey after Treaty of Lausanne.

V. THE INTERNATIONAL DIMENSION

The problem of Cyprus has had a ripple effect on NATO and other Western interests in the region. Following World War II, the UK's dominant role in the eastern Mediterranean passed to the United States and NATO. A permanent American naval presence was established in 1946 and rapidly grew into a two carrier task force, the Sixth Fleet. Greece and Turkey became members of the Alliance in 1952, and Washington entered into bilateral agreements with both countries to establish port facilities, airfields, communications centres and intelligence-gathering sites on their territories.[1] These enhanced America's capability to reinforce Greece and Turkey and their role within the Alliance but also aided projection of US interests in the region as a whole.[2]

The role and status of military facilities on Cyprus has been ambiguous, seemingly purposely so. British installations and forces there have never been NATO-assigned but their presence has been expressly described as being in the Alliance's interest as well as that of the UK.[3] The American Central Intelligence Agency (CIA) constructed monitoring stations on the island in 1949 under an agreement with the UK and these continued to function even after the island gained independence.[4] During their negotiations over Cypriot independence in 1959, Greece and Turkey agreed that they would support NATO membership for the new republic but, such was their mutual suspicion, they also stipulated that the installation of any NATO base and the composition of its forces would require their prior accord.[5] Archbishop Makarios claimed that before he joined the Non-Aligned Movement he sounded US officials about the desirability of Cypriot membership of NATO but was 'summarily' turned down.[6]

The US tended to be dismissive of Greco-Turkish nationalist concerns in the disputes over Cyprus, seeing these as irrelevant to the West's larger strategic interests on NATO's south-eastern flank. Among the political leadership in Greece and Turkey this created a feeling that their countries were being treated as client states rather than allies. Their disillusionment coincided with the emergence in the 1960s of the 'new left', propounding Marxist doctrines but not allegiance to the Soviet Union. The combination of these factors caused questions to be raised in both Greece and Turkey about the merits of membership of NATO and this, in turn, made the American bases in both countries a focus for dissent.

The Turkish government sought to exercise greater authority over US activities, and in 1969 the bases were brought under the aegis of a Defence Co-operation Agreement (DCA) which stressed their use for NATO purposes or for jointly-agreed activities. Nevertheless, left-wing agitation against the US and the Alliance grew so intense that visits to Turkish ports by vessels of the Sixth Fleet had to be halted because the safety of crew members ashore could not be guaranteed.

In Greece, the Colonels' dictatorship (1967–74) suppressed such overt antipathy. The Johnson Administration applied a perfunctory heavy-arms embargo to demonstrate its distaste for dictatorship, although during the years this was in force (1967–70) there were more military supplies transferred to Greece than in the three years prior to the coup.[7] The Nixon Administration openly co-operated with the regime,[8] valuing the apparent stability it afforded in an otherwise turbulent area.[9] US Defense Secretary Melvin Laird and Vice President Spiro Agnew visited Greece and in 1973 a homeporting agreement was signed for the destroyer squadron of the Sixth Fleet, providing for the settlement of more than 3,000 servicemen and their dependents.[10]

The belief grew throughout the Greek political spectrum that the junta was sanctioned by Washington in the hope of securing a settlement on Cyprus along the lines of the Acheson plan. Received wisdom among Greeks and Greek-Cypriots is that when in 1974 Brigadier Ioannides acted to depose Makarios, he believed he had struck a tacit bargain through CIA contacts to secure *enosis* in exchange for granting a Turkish military presence on the island. The Greeks convinced themselves that America would prevent a Turkish invasion as it had done in 1964 and 1967.

US Secretary of State Henry Kissinger has disclaimed being party to any such deal. He has written that he was too preoccupied with Watergate and the aftermath of the October 1973 Arab–Israeli war to pay proper attention to Cyprus. Nevertheless, US State Department staff had reported the likelihood that Greece would attempt to overthrow Makarios well before it happened,[11] and the scenario of a coup followed by a Turkish landing was predicted in remarkably prescient detail in both the Cypriot and American press months before the event.[12] Thus, Kissinger must at least have been aware of the prospect. He believed in the value of a controlled crisis to resolve an impasse provided, of course, that he could contain the complications. This presumably accounts for the appointment just three months before the coup of a new US ambassador to Cyprus of remarkably high standing, former Deputy Assistant Secretary of State Rodger Davis. He would have been responsible for overseeing the aftermath of events had he not been assassinated just days after the second Turkish landing.

Kissinger was instrumental in securing the July cease-fire[13] and in persuading Ankara to consider, during the Geneva talks, the possibility of a cantonal federation.[14] His overriding concern, however, was to prevent military escalation which might provoke a war between Greece and Turkey[15] and he rejected a proposal made by British Foreign Secretary James Callaghan during the cease-fire hiatus, that the UK should reinforce its UN contingent and seek the authority of the Security Council for UNFICYP 'to stand astride any Turkish line of advance. . . .'. Callaghan argued that such a contingency plan might just deter a second Turkish attack but Kissinger believed that '. . . even to focus on this eventuality would influence events to move onto a military plane'. Callaghan considered Kissinger to be 'mistaken', but the UK government, ever mindful of the fiasco which had resulted from the divergence between UK and US views over Suez, declined as a consequence to exercise its guarantor role by military action.[16]

Greek-Turkish relations

At the time of the invasion, Greece and Turkey were already in dispute over territorial waters and seabed rights in the Aegean Sea. Greece sought to extend its six-mile territorial waters to 12 miles which Turkey said would block free passage from its western ports to the Mediterranean and constitute a cause for war. Greece insists that each Aegean island has its own continental shelf, giving it control over the greater part of the seabed, while Turkey argues the case for natural prolongation of its mainland shelf.[17] NATO had intervened once already in 1974 to forestall hostilities over Turkish oil exploration.

Cyprus therefore merely aggravated what was already a volatile situation. The political government restored in Greece redeployed some 30,000 troops with associated armour to islands in the eastern Aegean.[18] These were forces of the Attika and the Islands command, traditionally not assigned to NATO. A squadron of F-5 aircraft was stationed on Lemnos at the mouth of the Dardanelles, and other tourist airports were hardened to take military aircraft. The airfields run in a north-south line through the Aegean from Kavalla on the mainland to the islands of Skyros, Thera, Karpathos and Rhodes.[19] Shore defences have been improved and new equipment acquired to ensure resupply capacity.

In 1975, Turkey created the Fourth Army which also is not assigned to NATO. Headquartered at Izmir, it is known colloquially as the Aegean Army. Its structure and status are not clear. In 1976 its commander described it as a force of 123,000 men with 'striking capability'.[20] In 1984, however, NATO parliamentarians were told it never consisted of more than 30,000 conscripts and that it was 'unthinkable' that the units could fulfil a combat role.[21] Air force training takes place at Izmir and, though there is no naval base at the port, landing craft are stationed nearby. Military aircraft flying from airfields in western Turkey could attack targets throughout the entire Aegean basin. Greek military authorities claim that, in total, the Turkish manpower and armaments in the region constitute a potential invasion force of 150,000 men, backed up by helicopters, transport planes and naval assault craft. The conflicting Greek and Turkish appreciations of the Turkish troop strengths need not be mutually exclusive.

Turkey complains that militarization of the islands by Greece is in breach of long-standing treaty obligations. The 1923 Treaty of Lausanne provided that there should be only security forces, not armed forces, on the Greek islands (Lemnos and Samothrace) and the Turkish islands (Gökçeada, Bozcaada and Lagoussai) at the mouth of the Dardanelles; and only 'persons locally recruited for their military service' on the four Greek islands closest to the Turkish coast, Lesbos, Chios, Samos and Ikaria.[22]

Greece claims that the 1936 Montreux Convention allowed for remilitarization of the islands of the Straits. This was undertaken by Turkey in 1936 and the following year Greece declared Lemnos to be a 'fortified island under surveillance'.[23] The debate about the legality of the militarization of Lemnos hinges upon interpretation of the preamble to the Montreux Convention and whether or not the convention replaces the Treaty of Lausanne. Greece also adduces secondary texts which it claims give practical force to its case. Its arguments over the islands of the Straits are the more persuasive.[24] However, the legality of the concentration of Greek forces on the other islands mentioned in the Treaty of Lausanne is questionable.

The 1946 Treaty of Paris, by which Italy assigned Greece the Dodecanese islands, specified that these too should be demilitarized. Greece breached this condition when, after the invasion of Cyprus by Turkish forces, it garrisoned the islands and reinforced their coastal defences. Greece argues, however, that confronted with the Aegean Army, it has an overriding right of legitimate self-defence under Article 51 of the UN charter. Ankara counters that the charter is meant only to apply in the event of aggression and that, since there has been none against Greece, this is a distortion of its true meaning. Greece notes that Turkey had declared its intention to establish the Aegean Army before Greek garrisons were established on the Dodecanese islands and it makes the further political point that the provision of adequate defence for areas of its sovereign territory is simply common sense.

Since January 1985, Greece has proclaimed what it calls a New Defence Doctrine. Military authorities say that they subscribe to the Alliance threat analysis that the Warsaw Pact is the potential enemy, but simultaneously assert that Greece's only bellicose neighbour is Turkey, hence the primary threat perception has been 'reoriented'.[25] Officials are purposely ambiguous about the practical effects of the policy. They insist that no new units have been created. However, recent weapons acquisitions, while consistent with a general programme of armaments modernization, have included equipment that would be particularly suitable for Aegean defence. The navy has acquired modern 209-class submarines, *Combattante* patrol boats armed with anti-ship missiles and new frigates. Heavy-lift helicopters have been purchased for troop reinforcement and resupply, and radar capabilities have been improved. Similarly, Turkey has acquired new submarines and *Kartal*-class patrol boats and embarked upon a new frigate building programme.

Relations with NATO

Prime Minister Karamanlis' withdrawal of Greek forces from NATO's integrated military structure in 1974 was designed to emphasize to

Greece's allies the importance which Athens attached to Cyprus.[26] It was a decision taken with great reluctance. Greek officers left the joint land and air headquarters at Izmir immediately, but it was not until a year later that the legal procedures for withdrawal were instituted.

By 1977, however, Athens had concluded that the advantages which were accruing to Turkey within NATO outweighed any leverage that could be gained by continued Greek withdrawal, and in June that year the government proposed reintegration. Its terms were the establishment of separate land and air commands at Larissa – Allied Land Forces South-Central (LANDSOUTHCENT) and the Seventh Allied Tactical Air Force (SEVENATAF)[27] respectively – and restoration of the *status quo ante* 1974 as regards operational responsibilities in the Aegean. Turkey did not object to the creation of the new headquarters but had reservations about the proposed operational arrangements.

Prior to 1974, Greece had been responsible for air defence up to the eastern boundary of the Athens civil flight information region (FIR) and for naval operations outside Turkish territorial waters. That is to say Greece was responsible for the whole of the Aegean west of Turkey's six-mile limit or the median line in the case of the narrower channels between the eastern islands and the mainland. After its withdrawal Greece became responsible only for its own territorial waters and airspace. Greece felt that, as it was returning to the Alliance without there having been any move on Turkey's part to withdraw troops from Cyprus, it should not be expected to pay any price for re-entry. Ankara, for its part, complained that the Allies, in their eagerness to reincorporate Greece, were prepared to act without adequate consideration of Turkey's security concerns.

Turkey points out, for example, that the outer limit of the Athens FIR is just one minute's flying time off the Turkish coast. It argues that to confine its air force to operations within such a limited area would not only constrain its defensive capabilities against Warsaw Pact air intruders but could also expose it to surprise attack from Greece.[28] Turkey seeks command arrangements which either give it greater responsibility or which leave operational boundaries relatively undefined.[29] Greece says it is unthinkable that Turkey should have defence responsibilities west of the eastern Greek islands. It asserts that this would be militarily and politically unreasonable even were relations impeccable and that it is impossible in the light of outstanding disputes.

Negotiations for Greek reintegration within the Alliance dragged on over three years, with successive agreements between Athens and NATO authorities in Brussels being vetoed by Ankara. Finally, in October 1980, just a month after the military seized power in Turkey, the Generals' regime agreed to terms adumbrated in a memorandum drafted by the then SACEUR, General Bernard Rogers.[30] This stipulated that re-entry affected only NATO military activities and had no bearing on other issues pending between Greece and Turkey. The separate headquarters were to be established and the Sixth (Turkish) and Seventh (Greek) tactical air forces were to consult with Commander, Allied Air Forces Southern Europe (COMAIRSOUTH) in Naples, Italy, to arrange 'for an integrated system of air defense'. The Commander-in-Chief Allied Forces Southern Europe (CINCSOUTH), also based in Naples, was to determine delegation of naval control.

Talks intended to lead to implementation of the agreement failed to satisfy either side and eventually were abandoned. Greece decided not to establish either LANDSOUTHCENT or SEVENATAF until terms of reference governing their missions and responsibilities were agreed. Turkey says that it feels cheated, since an understanding that Greece would come to some accommodation was implicit in the setting aside of its veto on Greek reintegration. NATO authorities are sympathetic to this view.

Greece refuses to participate in major NATO exercises in the Aegean. The ostensible reason is the failure of commanders to include the island of Lemnos. Greece argues that Lemnos, together with other Aegean islands, constitutes a strategic second line of defence against Soviet vessels exiting the Black Sea via the Straits. It has offered to assign the forces stationed there to NATO. Turkey sees this as an attempt to justify the 'illegal' fortification of the islands and has vetoed the assignment.

Joseph Luns, the then Secretary General, ruled that NATO should not become involved in the bilateral dispute. He also determined that there should be no infrastructure funding for Lemnos and that commanders should not include it in exercises. Greece maintains that this constitutes bias rather than even-handedness[31] and says it will refuse to participate in joint Aegean exercises until the island is incorporated.[32] The autumn manoeuvres, *Display Determination*, and some lesser exercises have gone ahead regardless in international and Turkish territorial waters. Greece claims that this compromises its arguments about operational responsibility and says that commanders are *de facto* intervening in a political dispute between member states. Greek irritation is aggravated by the fact that neither Turkish nor US military aircraft recognize a ten-mile territorial airspace limit which was proclaimed in 1931.[33] During exercises Greece regularly scrambles and intercepts such intruders and has issued a persistent stream of diplomatic protests.

Greek reaction has escalated over the years. First, Athens said it was prepared to take part in NATO exercises in the Cretan and Ionian Seas provided there was a moratorium on exercises in the Aegean. When this failed to produce the desired response, Greece refused to participate in any Aegean exercises. Subsequently it denied the use of NATO infrastructure facilities to forces taking part in exercises in which it did not participate.

To prevent forces stationed on Lemnos being assigned to NATO, Turkey has, since 1983, vetoed the entire Greek response to the annual planning questionnaire for NATO's Defence Review Committee (DRC). Turkish diplomats argue that military merit is not relevant, merely the matter of law. Greece has retaliated by counter-vetoing the Turkish reply, openly acknowledging that this is a political act. These mutual vetoes of each others 'country chapters' means that technically neither Greece nor Turkey has forces committed to the Alliance, which complicates SACEUR's planning. The dispute about whether Greece has a right to fortify its eastern Aegean islands has also led to mutual vetoes on NATO infrastructure spending programmes worth hundreds of millions of dollars.

Bilateral base accords
Cyprus similarly provided a spur to disputes between the south-eastern flank Allies and the United States. Under strong popular pressure, the Karamanlis Government undertook in 1975 to review bilateral military agreements with a view to the 'elimination, consolidation and reduction' of the bases. Those which remained were to be placed under Greek commanders in order to ensure that operations served national interests. The Sixth Fleet homeport facilities were cancelled and a decision was taken to close Athens Hellenikon airbase although it was not implemented. Given the Greek perception of US complicity in the partition of Cyprus, the government might have been expected to have acted more vigorously against the bases and to have limited its action against NATO. However, it could not afford to lose the military assistance which flowed from the presence of the bases and which helped to sustain the balance of power with Turkey. Moreover, there was a strong Greek-American lobby in the US Congress and it was felt this could be used to exert pressure on Turkey. Athens adopted a posture designed to demonstrate its displeasure with the Pentagon and the Administration, while endeavouring not to alienate Congress.

In February 1975 Congress imposed an embargo on arms shipments to Turkey on the grounds that American equipment had been misused in the Cyprus landing. The laws governing arms aid stipulate that it is furnished solely for internal security and self-defence. The embargo stopped the delivery of arms already purchased by Turkey, the disbursement of $200 m in grants and the transfer of a further $1 bn in matériel surplus from the US forces withdrawn from Vietnam. The action was vigorously opposed by the US administration, particularly by Secretary of State Kissinger, who argued that it would seriously weaken Turkey's defensive capability and thus damage the Alliance.

The action infuriated Turkey's pro-western political elite which felt it already faced sufficient difficulties in supporting the country's commitment to NATO in the face of left-wing political criticism. More tellingly, the gesture raised doubts, reminiscent of those engendered by the Johnson letter in 1964, about America's overall commitment to the defence of Turkey. Ankara retaliated by abrogating the 1969 DCA and placing US installations under the control of the Turkish armed forces. Four major intelligence-gathering facilities, said to provide the US with up to a quarter of its raw data on the Soviet Union, were closed and remained so until after the embargo was lifted in September 1978.

In 1976, the Ford Administration hastened to negotiate four-year base agreements with both nations. Preliminary agreement was reached with Turkey for the use of 26 installations in exchange for $1 bn-worth of military aid, and with Greece for the use of four major and a dozen minor sites coupled with $700 m-worth of aid. In an accompanying letter, Dr Kissinger offered the Greek government a cautious security guarantee and promised to pursue 'just territorial arrangements' in Cyprus.[34] The incoming Carter Administration decided, however, not to ask Congress to ratify the Turkish DCA until Ankara had made moves towards a settlement, and both the agreements eventually lapsed. Nevertheless, the concept was established of a 10:7 ratio in US aid to Turkey and Greece and, despite objections by successive administrations, it has since been maintained by Congress.

Turkey refused to make concessions under duress and, in April 1978, President Carter finally asked Congress to lift the embargo as a prelude to that summer's initiative on Cyprus. Congress initially refused. This decision was reversed, however, after Prime Minister Bulent Ecevit received the Soviet Chief of Staff in Ankara and discussed military co-operation and the possibility of arms sales with him.

The US bases in Turkey re-opened in October 1978 and, after a year's negotiations, a new Defence and Economic Co-operation Agreement (DECA) came into effect in 1980, designed to cover the period up until 1985. It provided for US participation in 'joint defense measures' at 12 designated bases, while stressing that 'the defense co-operation envisaged . . . shall be limited to obligations arising out of the North Atlantic Treaty'.[35] Unilateral use of the bases by the US, particularly in support of its Middle East policies, would require prior Turkish agreement. In the throes of an economic crisis, Turkey demanded greater financial assistance, including more grant aid. The Administration, mindful of Congressional constraints, was only able to commit itself to provide assistance on 'the best terms as may be possible',[36] though it did embark upon joint weapons upgrade and production programmes to help modernize the aged Turkish armoury. Negotiations begun in 1985 to renew the Turkish DECA stalled over financial arrangements and dragged on until May 1987, when it was decided to extend the existing agreement till the end of the decade, with the associated economic matters consigned to a side-letter. Ratification was delayed a further eight months after Congress slashed the Administration's 1988 military assistance request by more than 40 per cent in order to sustain the 10:7 ratio between aid to Turkey and Greece.

The negotiation of a DECA for Greece bogged down in domestic Greek politics, and the bases appeared to be in jeopardy when the socialists (PASOK) were elected in 1981 with a mandate to close them.

Once in office, however, Prime Minister Andreas Papandreou succumbed to the aid rationale, and in 1983 his government concluded a five-year DECA covering four major bases and a number of minor facilities. Policy at the time was to project the bases as serving solely American interests, and the agreement pointedly made no reference to their having NATO functions. The deal was portrayed in Greece as providing for closure of the bases when the DECA expired on 31 December 1988.

After much preliminary posturing and manoeuvring, however, negotiations opened in November 1987 for a new DECA, and latterly official policy has stressed the importance of Greece's contribution to the Alliance in playing host to these facilities. The government set as a condition that the new agreement should advance Greek interests over the Aegean and Cyprus. US officials said that they could not make specific commitments on these issues but that they would endeavour to maintain the balance of power in the region. In July 1988, the Greek government gave formal notice of termination of the 1983 DECA meaning that, if no new agreement is reached the US will have to leave the bases by the end of May 1990. Prime Minister Papandreou promised that any new accord would be put to the public in a referendum.[37]

The Davos process
In March 1987, a confrontation over proposed Greek oil exploration outside six-mile waters, caused both Athens and Ankara to put their armed forces on alert. The incident was sufficiently acute for NATO permanent representatives to convene in emergency session and to call upon the two sides to 'avoid recourse to force at all cost'.[38] The incident was defused by a tacit, mutual agreement not to drill in contested areas. Prior to this Prime Minister Papandreou had said there could be no talks with Turkey on any outstanding differences so long as Turkish troops remained in Cyprus. The imminence of war apparently shocked him into an awareness of the need for dialogue.

An exchange of diplomatic notes between Papandreou and Turkish Prime Minister Turgut Ozal led to a meeting in January 1988 in the margins of an international economic conference at Davos in Switzerland. The two men concluded what they termed a 'no-war' agreement.[39] Effectively, they agreed to set aside their differences in the Aegean and to introduce confidence-building measures which might create the climate which would allow their eventual resolution. They agreed to establish a hot-line between the two capitals and to set up two committees: one to explore areas of political co-operation and another to pursue economic, social and cultural collaboration. As an initial gesture of goodwill, Ankara revoked a decree, passed during the Cyprus crisis of 1964, which froze the property assets of the Greek minority resident in Turkey. This affected some $300 million-worth of property belonging to some 12,000 individuals. In exchange, Greece agreed to sign protocols by which it ratified the 1964 Turkish Association Agreement with the European Community, though it insisted this did not affect its opposition to full Turkish membership so long as occupation troops remain in Cyprus.

In May 1988, the political committee concluded an agreement about the conduct of military exercises in the Aegean, designed to eliminate contentious practices.[40] Coincidentally the two nations agreed to lift their mutual vetoes on certain NATO infrastructure projects[41] although they were soon to return to the practice of reciprocal blocking votes. At a subsequent meeting in September 1988, the Foreign Ministers of the two nations drafted a document containing 'guidelines for the prevention of accidents or incidents on the open seas and in international airspace'.[42] No further details were given at the time, but if the document provides the basis of 'rules of the road' in the Aegean then it could constitute a major step towards defusing tensions.[43]

Cyprus was deemed to be a matter for the UN and not for the bilateral agenda. However, Papandreou insisted that the presence of the Turkish troops on the island was a matter which concerned Greece as a guarantor, as a member of the UN and as the metropolis of Hellenism. Ozal agreed to hear him out but not to discuss the troop presence except in the context of a total settlement package for the island. The issue was raised at a meeting between the two men in Athens in June 1988 after which Ozal said that the troops would not remain on the island indefinitely.[44] The tenor and context of his remarks could have been construed as suggesting a relaxation in the previous adamantine determination to maintain a permanent garrison on the island. Papandreou allowed that he saw 'a light at the end of the tunnel'.[45]

The British factor
The role of the UK in Cyprus has been largely self-serving. As was the case in many other of its colonies, it retained control long after logic dictated that self-government was in order, at the cost of a needless guerrilla war. The reluctance with which the island was relinquished was symbolized by the Treaty of Establishment which provided that the Republic consisted of that territory which did not remain British. This legal nicety meant that, as the Sovereign Base Areas have never formed part of the Republic, no rent has ever been paid.[46]

The bases comprise three per cent of the island. They are styled British Dependent Territories and have their own three-mile territorial waters and airspace. Since they are military bases, the Commander British Forces Cyprus is also administrator with executive and legislative authority. The 1960 agreements incorporated a further 31 reserved areas – ranging from off-base radar sites to water sources – of which 15 are still under British jurisdiction.[47] There is a large airfield at Akrotiri, a smaller strip at Dhekelia and a helicopter base at Episkopi within the eastern SBA. Other facilities include a port at Akrotiri adequate for frigates, vital radar facilities at Mount Olympus in the Troodos mountains, an array of signals intelligence and relay facilities, a satellite station, and a major radio relay station operated by BBC External Services but controlled by the Foreign and Commonwealth Office.

In the 1960s and early 1970s, the bases functioned within the context of the UK's commitment to CENTO, with two squadrons of nuclear strike bombers and a squadron of fighter support. Following defence reviews in the late 1970s, operational flying from the Akrotiri base ceased and it became a major training facility for RAF units. The SBAs also provide training facilities for land forces on rotation from the UK and Gibraltar. The more important role of the bases today is intelligence-gathering and signals relay. Large antennae farms form part of a global network stretching from the US and Canada eastwards through the UK to Australia. From Cyprus, intercepts are made of aircraft, ship and satellite communications in an arc from Libya through the Middle East to Iran and the Black Sea basin. The information is exchanged with the American National Security Agency and is a major contribution to the US–UK defence relationship.

The location of the bases, in the middle of the prime area of operations of Soviet Naval Forces in the Mediterranean (the Fifth Eskadra, known in NATO terminology as SOVMEDRON), makes them invaluable to the Alliance. Because of the delicacy of the relationship with the non-aligned Republic, UK authorities insist that the bases have no formal NATO role, although they do acknowledge that their maintenance is in the interests of the Alliance.[48]

The bases have frequently provided logistic support for US forces operating in the Middle East in a peacekeeping role. For example, they provided back-up support for the sweeping of mines from the Suez canal in 1974, and logistic and communications support for the Multinational Force in Lebanon in 1982. U-2 aircraft have flown from Akrotiri since the 1970s to monitor the cease-fire in the Sinai.[49]

The importance of the bases to UK and Western security interests has compromised the UK's performance of its role as guarantor. Technically, it is no part of the purpose of the bases that they be used for implementation of the Treaty of Guarantee. They are intended solely to secure British security interests.[50] In practice, however, limited numbers of forces have been deployed from the bases to perform peacekeeping functions. In 1963, UK troops formed a Truce Force to secure the cease-fire, and British soldiers have always formed the largest contingent in UNFICYP. The bases provide the majority of UNFICYP's logistic support. In 1974, British troops reinforced the contingent at Nicosia airport to ensure it was not overrun by massing Turkish armour.

The ambiguity, arising from the fact that the bases are not intended to perform any domestic function but nevertheless have contributed to maintaining the peace on the island, has led to confusion about the British role as guarantor. The Treaty of Guarantee obliges the UK to take joint action with Greece and Turkey but also affords it a legal

65

right to take unilateral action to preserve the independence, territorial integrity and constitution of the Republic. The House of Commons Select Committee in 1976 argued that, confronted with the Greek coup and the Turkish invasion, the UK had a moral obligation to use its right to intervene.[51] Yet in both 1963 and 1974, the UK sought to diffuse its guarantee responsibility so as to lower its profile and thus not jeopardize the SBAs. In 1963, after convening the abortive London talks between the Greek- and Turkish-Cypriots, the UK appealed first to the US and NATO for peacekeeping assistance and later to the UN. In 1974, after unsuccessful efforts to mediate between Ecevit and Ioannides, the Wilson Government opted for UK forces to operate only under UN colours.

In 1963, the UK still had the resources to go beyond its interposition of forces on the Green Line in Nicosia and to impose more widespread order, but only by the sort of large-scale troop commitment it had sought to escape by granting independence in the first place. To have returned in strength would have carried with it the risk of inviting international repercussions by appearing to be re-occupying the island. Field Marshal Lord Carver, who was then Commander of the Truce Force on the island, has written that Britain was 'anxious to spread the load' and viewed NATO, of which the other guarantors were also members, as the obvious alternative.[52] When this met with resistance from Makarios, the UK turned to the UN.

In 1974, the British Labour government and the Chief of the Defence Staff (Lord Carver again) decided that the UK did not have the resources to take successful unilateral action.[53] Ecevit asked to land Turkish forces via the bases,[54] and Karamanlis sought British air cover for a convoy to land Greek troops. Both were refused. The Wilson Government rationalized its posture by arguing that co-operation with Turkey would not have restored the *status quo* as conceived by the Greek-Cypriots and would have alienated the majority population on the island, while assisting Greek forces to land would almost certainly have led to war between the two allies in the name of a Cypriot constitution which had been a dead letter for the past eleven years.

Having determined not to take unilateral military action, the UK opted for measures designed to secure the bases and perhaps deter Turkey. The SBAs were reinforced with 2,645 men, including two Royal Marine commando groups, and with eight ground-attack *Phantom* jets. The helicopter carrier *Hermes* was diverted to Cyprus the day following the Greek coup, where it was joined by a cruiser, a guided missile destroyer, two frigates and a submarine.[55] In the event, however, the warships were not used to deter the Turkish landings, being employed only to evacuate refugees, although they had to confront Turkish forces to accomplish this.[56] Despite Callaghan's belief that Turkey would have backed down if faced with determined opposition, he could not be certain of this without American backing, and the UK government was not prepared to risk war with Turkey for fear of the consequences for NATO. Hence the UK confined itself to political and diplomatic initiatives.

As a consequence, British influence has been much diminished with the Cyprus government. The Greek-Cypriots continue to tolerate the bases because of their substantial input into the southern economy and because they provide a form of negative guarantee against the possibility of Turkey one day overrunning the whole of the island. Greek-Cypriot parties of the left are committed to the removal of the SBAs, and President Vassiliou has said that he would like to see them go eventually. But he acknowledges that their departure 'is not something that depends on us'.[57]

Soviet involvement

Moscow's principal concern in the south-east is the maintenance of egress from Soviet warm water Black Sea ports to the Mediterranean via the Dardanelles. Its Cyprus policy has always been subordinated to this larger consideration and, as a consequence, has been subject to fluctuations as it has sought to capitalize on the dissension which disputes on the island have provoked between NATO allies. However, Soviet policy has been consistent in two broad objectives: to prevent incorporation of the island into the Alliance; and to secure British withdrawal from the SBAs.[58]

Moscow recognizes that Cyprus is non-aligned within the Western camp in much the same way that Yugoslavia is non-aligned within the Eastern sphere of influence, and has accordingly counselled AKEL to assume the role of power-broker rather than to look to take office itself. AKEL, in the main, has readily adapted to the frequent adjustments in the Soviet Union's Cyprus policy and, over the course of the 40 years that the party was under the leadership of Ezekias Papaioannou, Moscow came to take the party somewhat for granted. It remains to be seen whether this will change under AKEL's new leader Demetris Christofias.

At the international level, the Soviet Union has sought on the one hand to frustrate developments which might lead to partition and union of the two territories with Greece and Turkey, while on the other hand, it has sought to take advantage of the disappointment and disaffection with the West engendered in the respective mainland populations by the frustration of their aspirations to achieve *enosis* or *taksim*.

This was most apparent in the mid-1960s. Khrushchev sent letters to the major powers warning against the introduction of a NATO force into the island. Makarios appealed to the USSR for help against Turkish invasion threats and Moscow supplied him with arms including surface-to-air missiles.[59] But as Ankara agonized over its future defence relationship with the West in the wake of the Johnson letter of June 1964,[60] Moscow began to court Turkey and, during the period from 1965 to 1967 when *enosis* was still a live concern for many Greek-Cypriots, the Soviet Union shifted towards recognition of the two communities in Cyprus. Ultimately, it stopped its shipments of arms to Makarios and, publicly at least, condemned consignments from Czechoslovakia.

The Soviet Union was one of the first nations to recognize the Papadopoulos dictatorship in Greece, although it denounced the machinations against Makarios of unionists connected with the military-backed regime in Athens. In Turkey, it succoured the left-wing groups which fomented the disturbances against the US presence in the late 1960s, which, in turn, contributed to the situation that prompted the military intervention of 1971.

After the US arms embargo on Turkey in 1975, the Soviet Union took advantage of Ankara's estrangement from Washington to invest heavily in Turkish industry and offered the prospect of military co-operation. In Greece, it sought good relations with the restored civilian government, offering cheap fuel during the oil price crises and again proposing joint large-scale investment projects. It even placed contracts for the repair of support vessels of the Fifth Eskadra with Greek shipyards.

The Soviet Union objected to the despatch of the UN peacekeeping force to Cyprus yet has consistently promoted the international body as the forum best suited to resolve the inter-communal problems. Since the division of the island Moscow has continued to recognize the Greek-Cypriots as the legitimate government of the island as a whole, while assiduously acknowledging the existence of two distinct communities, both of whose interests must be taken into account in the final solution. It has espoused separation of domestic matters, which it says should be solved between the two communities, from the international aspects of the problem, such as demilitarization and security guarantees.

In its most recent initiative, in 1986, it circulated a document in the UN General Assembly and the Security Council calling for an international conference involving the permanent members of the Security Council, Greece, Turkey, representatives of the two communities, and delegates from non-aligned nations.[61] This supported a unified state and insisted that division or 'absorbsion (sic), full or partial, by any country or countries are inadmissible'. It said that demilitarization was essential to a settlement, and that use of the island for military purposes by other states was also 'inadmissible'. As well as being anxious about the SBAs, Soviet officials have been very concerned that the airfield at Geçitkale might be used by the US Central Command in the event of conflict in the Middle East. The proposal called for all foreign troops to be withdrawn and foreign bases to be dismantled. The guarantors of a settlement should include Greece and Turkey but also members of the Security Council and the non-aligned nations. Their terms of reference should 'exclude the possibility of future outside interference. . . .'

The proposal for an international conference found favour with Athens and the Greek-Cypriot leadership but was dismissed by Ankara and the Turkish-Cypriots. Kyprianou pressed Pérez de Cuéllar to persuade members of the UN Security Council of its desirability, but the Secretary General reported, not unexpectedly, that he found them divided about the idea. Over the next 18 months, there was intense diplomatic activity between Moscow and Nicosia, and the Greek-Cypriots had high hopes of Soviet promotion, at the autumn 1987 General Assembly, of another resolution which would have helped to shore up their role as the sole legitimate government. In the event this did not materialize, and pursuit of the resolution was abandoned after the presidential elections which brought Vassiliou to power.

The Greek-Cypriots sought unsuccessfully to have the Cyprus question formally incorporated on the agenda of the Reagan–Gorbachev summits. Significantly, however, the level of Soviet attention to Cyprus has abated as both super-powers have moved to de-escalate confrontation in other areas of interest.

EEC relations

In June 1973, Cyprus entered into an Association Agreement with the European Economic Community with a view to establishing a Customs Union within a decade. The move was necessary to offset the adverse effects of the loss of Commonwealth preference following the accession to the Community earlier that year of the United Kingdom, its main trading partner. The Agreement called for a gradual reduction in tariffs on both sides in two five-year phases, but the process was disrupted by the Turkish invasion.

The Nine expressed grave concern over the sequence of events in summer 1974 and called for a negotiated settlement between the two communities. The Community adopted the policy that its Association Agreement was legally with the internationally-recognized government of Cyprus but that trade and other arrangements flowing from it should apply to the entire population of the island. For example, the Community stipulated that financial assistance provided under two aid protocols should be disbursed to the common good and that the funds should be spent on projects such as joint sewerage, electricity and water supplies. The Turkish-Cypriots complained that these were of greater benefit to the southern territory and argued that they should be allowed to invest their portion of the funds on infrastructure projects of their own choosing in the north. The Community insisted on its point of view and the joint works went ahead.

After the Turkish-Cypriot declaration of independence, the government of the Republic issued new customs documentation and argued that only goods accompanied by these papers should benefit from preferential tariff treatment under the Association Agreement. The Commission noted the legality of its position but the Council of Ministers ignored it after individual member states invoked the common benefit provisions. Member nations, particularly West Germany and the UK, continued to trade with the northern territory. The latter is its principal trading partner after Turkey and takes more of the agricultural exports of the TRNC than even the mainland.

Efforts by the government of the Republic to initiate negotiations for the second stage of the Association Agreement met with constant foot-dragging by the Commission and the terms of the first phase were repeatedly extended. In European Political Co-operation (EPC) deliberations, the Community took no independent line on Cyprus but rather continued to endorse the efforts of the UN Secretary General to find a solution through inter-communal negotiations.

The accession of Greece to the EC in 1981 quickened awareness of the problem of Cyprus, though not immediately since the socialists, during their early years in office, were too busy rationalizing their own policy towards the Community. Following PASOK's re-election in 1985, however, Greece made Cyprus a priority issue, raising it regularly in Community fora. Ministers tended to hear out their Greek counterparts politely before moving on to other business.

In December 1985, as the UN Secretary General was preparing his Draft Framework Agreement, the EC Council issued a mandate to the Commission to commence negotiations with Cyprus for a Customs Union. That same month Turkey requested normalization of relations with the Community under its 1964 Association Agreement which had been frozen following the coup in 1980. There were objections from some member states that human rights and democratic institutions had not been fully restored, despite the election in November 1983 of a civilian government under the conservative Turgut Ozal. It was not, therefore, until September 1986 that the first Association Council was convened under the British presidency. In the following April, Turkey formally applied to become a full member. The application was forwarded to the Commission for an opinion – the first stage in the consideration of an application – although it was generally accepted that there was little likelihood of Turkish accession before the turn of the century and possibly for a decade beyond.

In May 1987, agreement was concluded with the Republic of Cyprus to proceed to a Customs Union by 2002. The Turkish-Cypriots objected strenuously that they were not party to the negotiations, although Commission officials had kept them informed about their progress. On 14 November 1988, following meetings with EC officials in Brussels, President Vassiliou announced that Cyprus would apply to become a full member of the Community after the completion of the internal market in 1992. He said the policy was not directly linked with a Cyprus settlement because he expected the application would take ten years to process and he wanted the Cyprus problem resolved before then.

The Greek camp believes that Turkey's desire to join the Community provides the best prospect in years for breaking the Cyprus deadlock. They emphasize the anomaly of the troops of an applicant country (Turkey) occupying a substantial portion of the territory of an associated member nation (Cyprus), thus denying the majority of that country's population such basic rights as freedom of movement. The Greek government has said that so long as Turkish troops remain on the island it will use all means at its disposal to block Ankara's application. Indeed, even as it has proceeded with the Davos process of *rapprochement* on bilateral matters, Greece has blocked an EC financial protocol which would have provided Ecu 600 m in financial aid to the beleaguered Turkish economy and persuaded the Council formally to adopt the position that 'the problem of Cyprus affects also the relations between the Community and Turkey'. The political implications of this latter move so incensed Ankara's representatives at the second ministerial level Association Council in May 1988 that the Turkish delegation withdrew from the meeting amid bitter public recriminations.

Conversely, Greek Prime Minister Andreas Papandreou is on record as saying that if Turkey were to withdraw its troops from Cyprus, Greece would support its application for EC membership.[62] Prime Minister Ozal, however, has insisted that he is not prepared to pay any political price for accession. That said, Ankara's persuasion of Denktash to enter into negotiations with Vassiliou without substantial preconditions has been seen as a gesture designed at least to appear willing to be accommodating.

For the moment, Greek obstruction of the Turkish application suits a majority of the 12 member nations of the Community and saves them from having to express their own objections. The bureaucratic and economic problems of incorporation would be enormous. Turkey's population, projected to reach 80 m by the turn of the century, would be the largest in the Community, with *per capita* income only a fraction of the EC average. Integration of the huge Turkish farming community within the Common Agricultural Policy could bankrupt the EC. Freedom of movement would create emigration problems such as those already experienced with the large guest-worker population in Germany. Liberals have deep reservations about the Turkish record on human rights, while conservatives express more fundamental racial and religious objections, claiming that the Muslim Turks are simply not European.

By contrast, the potential of the massive Turkish market and the wealth of the country's resources are not lost on those who view the Community principally from an economic perspective. The need to shore up Turkey's secular political elite against Islamic fundamentalism is a concern for those who would bind the country to the West for security reasons. Exclusion, it is argued, could cause Turkey to drift towards the Arab world and potentially towards neutralism. It is possible that, were these factors eventually perceived to outweigh objections, then membership might be granted without particular reference to Cyprus. In the past, Community institutions have kept studiously aloof from political involvement in international disputes between members, such as those between the UK and Spain over Gibraltar, Britain and Eire over Ulster, and Spain and France over the Basque country.

Implications for a solution

The various aspects of the international dimension discussed above constitute yet another range of factors affecting the desirability of, and the prospects for, a resolution of the Cyprus problem. Cyprus is not a direct concern of NATO, but the disputes between two of its constituent members over the island have severely disrupted the coherence of the south-eastern flank. Moreover, the dispute over the island has adversely affected relations between the United States and both Greece and Turkey, disrupting not only the American contribution to the Alliance but also the pursuit of other US interests in the Middle East. The Soviet Union has been quick to capitalize on these disputes in order to keep the Alliance off balance. A Cyprus settlement would not necessarily lead to resolution of the outstanding bilateral disputes between Greece and Turkey in the Aegean but it would assist.

More recently, the European Community has become involved with the parties to the dispute. While it has attempted to keep the problem at arm's length it will inevitably become increasingly caught up in Cypriot affairs. It is in the interests of Western Europe that an early solution to the impasse on the island be achieved in order that defence and economic co-operation proceed smoothly. There is thus a demonstrable need for greater involvement of European political leaders in seeking to facilitate the settlement process.

VI. CONCLUSIONS

The seemingly inevitable consequence of the dissolution of empires is internecine strife between members of disparate ethnic and religious communities who, as subjects, cohabited peaceably for want of the opportunity to express their differences. The British empire is a classic example. The division of Cyprus is but one case in point, and far from the worst when compared with the civil conflicts in newly independent nations in the Indian subcontinent and Africa. In Cyprus, the problem was exacerbated by the historical enmity between mainland Greeks and Turks engendered by centuries of occupation and wars of liberation and suppression.

The inhabitants of Cyprus ordinarily are placid, gentle people, their quotidian lives revolving around their families, their lands and their religion. Under British rule, the two ethnic communities lived in relative harmony. When it became apparent that the colonial structure was in the process of dissolution, however, nationalist zealots in Greece and in Turkey, and among the respective communities on the island, boiled to the surface to become promoters of internal division.

The United Kingdom was not as responsible as it had been in other former colonies for the artificial constitutional construct with which the nascent independent state of Cyprus was encumbered. The UK was confounded by the intensity of nationalist sentiments and essentially washed its hands of the problem, leaving resolution to the governments in Athens and Ankara and retreating to the Sovereign Bases to look out for its own interests. The 1960 constitution contributed to the division by differentiating, rather than amalgamating, the two peoples. Its power-sharing arrangements required moderate men capable of compromise in order to be operable. Extremists, who identified more with their ethnic origins than with their newfound Cypriot nationality, ensured such co-operation was not forthcoming.

The former EOKA guerrillas and their supporters were determined to seize control of the state in order to unite Cyprus with Greece. The Turkish-Cypriots make much of the unionists' so-called 'Akritas Plan' (described at Chapter I, note 23) with its programme to suppress the minority community, by violence if needs be. The fighters of TMT were equally determined to segregate the Turkish-Cypriots in order to partition the island and link up with Turkey. Both were encouraged by militant irredentists from the respective mainlands.

The impetus to division was compounded by the policies of the super-powers. At least a third, and probably more, of the population of Cyprus were communists and the flamboyant Archbishop Makarios became a prominent personality in the Non-Aligned Movement. The US, concerned about what it perceived as a security risk to the southeastern flank of NATO, was prepared to carve up Cyprus between Greece and Turkey who, at least nominally, were allies, and who were ostensibly closely wedded to West. The Soviet Union, never averse to fishing in troubled Alliance waters, shaped its Cyprus policy and its relations with the two mainland governments so as to encourage disenchantment in Athens and Ankara with the US and the West generally, in the hope of diminishing Greek and Turkish commitment to NATO.

Both communities on Cyprus have legitimate grievances against one another. The Turkish-Cypriots clearly suffered under the domination of the majority in the eleven years from 1963 to 1974.[1] The Greek-Cypriots not only took heavy casualties but suffered the psychological scars of rape, wanton destruction and expropriation at the hands of the invading Turkish troops.[2] There were massacres and other atrocities on both sides. Exact figures for casualties are difficult to establish. The Turkish-Cypriots claim more than 900 dead and missing.[3] Some 2,000 Turkish troops and an equal number of Greek-Cypriots became casualties in the 1974 fighting;[4] 1,600 Greek-Cypriots are missing. Even the peacekeepers have suffered, with 141 UNFICYP personnel having died since the force was first deployed in 1964.

A third of the population of the island have been made refugees. The cost in terms of dislocation, damage and lost production is incalculable. The bill for the peacekeeping operation alone has topped $2 bn, approximately $3,000 for each inhabitant of the island.

Turkey has achieved its objective of creating a buffer between itself and the Hellenes of Cyprus and, unless there is some spectacular improvement in its relations with Greece or some regional conflict which spills over into Cyprus bringing about reunification as a side effect, there seems little likelihood that the ethnic division of the island will be reversed.

The Greek-Cypriots are increasingly resigned to this and, as a consequence, the focus of their negotiating demands has narrowed. Initially, they sought reintegration under a unitary government. Today they accept the concept of a bi-communal federation and their concentration is more on increasing the size of the southern sector in order that the maximum number of refugees can return to their homes. They continue to insist, however, on the three freedoms: of movement, of ownership of property, and of the right of settlement, but acknowledge that these may have to be applied in phases in order to overcome Turkish-Cypriot fears of being swamped. The Greek-Cypriots are concerned that the federal government should have substantial authority and not be merely a redundant superstructure on top of two largely independent states. Above all, they are anxious to achieve security arrangements for the new state which will preclude outside intervention. They want the Turkish troops withdrawn and some form of multilateral guarantee which will ensure that they cannot return.

The Turkish-Cypriots for their part want to neutralize the three freedoms, though, as indicated earlier, their positions have varied over the course of years depending upon the prevailing political climate. Purported proposals put to the UN Secretary General in November 1988 suggest a firm line is being taken in this latest round of nego-

74

tiations. According to press and diplomatic reports – which officials of both sides will neither confirm nor deny – the Turkish-Cypriot administration allows that there should be freedom of movement, though it insists that specific individuals, particularly ex-EOKA fighters, should continue to be proscribed and liable to deportation should they endeavour to enter the northern territory. More importantly, the Turkish-Cypriots argue that all property claims should be settled prior to an agreement in order to provide a legal framework to prevent incidents involving individuals returning and seeking to repossess their former farms, factories and residences. The settlement would be achieved through a combination of swaps and compensation. Once all outstanding claims had been settled, the Greek-Cypriots would have a right of establishment – not resettlement – in the north. It is a nice distinction but one which asserts the Turkish-Cypriot primacy in their region. This right of establishment would only be introduced after 18 years, though this time-frame would be reviewed nine years after a settlement. Even once the rights of establishment were granted, the Turkish-Cypriots want the right to control the number of people who might settle in the northern territory as a whole or in any particular area of the region in order that their dominance not be diluted.

There continue to be political rifts within the Greek-Cypriot community but these are increasingly based on domestic considerations and less on the national issue. There is no longer any manifest desire for *enosis*, although there is some residual sympathy, particularly amongst the clergy. The children of the generation which fought for the narrow nationalist cause have a broader view of a future in Europe, while those who have returned from the diaspora caused by the troubles see their prospects in a global perspective. The election of George Vassiliou, with his European background and Middle Eastern interests, is indicative of the change. His increased emphasis on the economy is more in tune with the aspirations of the burgeoning Greek-Cypriot middle class than was the single-minded concentration on the national issue of his predecessor Spyros Kyprianou.

The Turkish-Cypriots luxuriate in a new-found sense of security and are enjoying their autonomy, as witnessed by their perfervid politicking. They do not look upon the Turkish troops as an army of occupation but rather as protectors and compatriots, and they would rather continue with the *status quo*, with all its attendant difficulties, than revert to a situation in which they were in any way again cast as minority.

They are, however, increasingly dissatisfied with the economic disparity between the two regions of the island. The south Nicosia skyline, with its soaring glass and concrete office blocks, compared with the nineteenth-century brick and stone buildings in the Turkish-Cypriot northern sector is a daily reminder of the economic gulf and the cause of growing envy. Part of the fiscal problems of the north stems from the fact that the authorities have sought to compensate by allowing relatively high levels of consumer spending instead of imposing a regime of austerity which might help to balance the books.

There is also increasing dissatisfaction with the lack of opportunity for meaningful opposition to the policies of Rauf Denktash and the succession of National Unity Party governments. Inasmuch as this is seen to be the product of mainland Turkish support for Denktash, there is concomitant disaffection. This continues to be more than off-set, however, by feelings of gratitude for what Turkey has done on behalf of the Turkish-Cypriots. A majority still feel that half a loaf is better than no bread, though there is increasing suspicion that their circumstances might be enhanced under a federation. Their concern is that it should be on terms which would sustain their sense of security.

The principal stumbling block to a settlement is Denktash. His think-ing is set in the mould of three decades ago. He professes to believe that the Greek-Cypriots still seek *enosis* and, while he pays lip-service to the idea of confederation, basically remains the separatist he was when he helped found TMT in the 1950s. The occasional strictures which his administration has imposed on political opponents suggest the men-tality of the *pasha* rather than the democrat he believes himself to be. His rhetoric harps on the past. There is no evidence that he has derived any personal advantage from his activities but he must also be prey to the psychological factor that he has nothing to gain from a settlement. Unless the notion of an alternating presidency is resurrected, there is no likelihood that he would ever be elected head of state, and he would be reduced from the status of 'president' of the independent TRNC to that of leader of a constituent part of the new sovereign entity.

The latest round of UN-sponsored inter-communal talks, which began in August 1988, has seen a marked departure in form from pre-vious initiatives. The two community leaders, Vassiliou and Denktash, have been meeting face to face at the residence of the Sec-retary General's special representative, Oscar Camilion. Virtually all previous negotiating instruments have been set aside, thus freeing their conversations from the accreted *minutiae* of the years of dis-cussions. There have been no agenda, no supporting staff present and no formal minutes kept of the meetings. The format is tantamount to recognition of Denktash as the peer of Vassiliou, a huge concession in Greek-Cypriot minds, particularly when viewed in the context of Kyprianou's unwillingness even to treat with Denktash except at the high-level meetings in 1979 and 1985. Denktash continues to insist, however, that Vassiliou should represent himself only as the leader of the Greek community of Cyprus and not as president of the Republic, with the connotations that has of Greek dominion over the island.

The UN search for a solution to the Cyprus problem over the course of the last quarter of a century is a monument to its tenacity. There are those who would argue, however, that it has become part of the problem; the repeated rounds of talks under its auspices having so refined the subtleties of the issues that the two sides have lost sight of the substance.

This overlooks the fact that the antagonists have so far been unwilling to address the core problems, namely that the majority in what was designed as a power-sharing state has taken to itself the title of the government of the whole, and that the minority has retaliated by creating a secessionist state with the support of foreign invasion forces. The bargain necessary to resolve the problem must ultimately be recognition of some form of Turkish-Cypriot autonomy in exchange for Turkish troop withdrawals, and neither of these issues has yet reached the negotiating table. Inasmuch as the UN has allowed the negotiations to stall on the preliminary questions of constitutional and territorial arrangements it may have removed the impetus to tackle the harder issues. By keeping the two sides talking, however, it has prevented recourse to hostilities and it still provides the most likely forum for a settlement.

If negotiations to form a federation fail, the Greek-Cypriot sector would be a viable entity as it stands. Its two greatest concerns would be water supply and the provision of adequate defence. The Turkish-Cypriot territory could be developed, but this would be a long-term process and it is unlikely that it would ever be wholly self-sufficient.

Nevertheless, the Denktash administration points out that there are 16 member states of the UN with populations smaller than that of the TRNC. This begs the question of international recognition. Over the course of years, nine Islamic nations have either voted against or abstained from voting on UN resolutions which acknowledged the Greek-Cypriots as the government of the Republic.[5] The late President Zia ul-Haq was on record as saying that were the Secretary General to abandon his efforts to find a settlement then Pakistan would recognize the TRNC, and at one stage the Sultanate of Brunei appeared to have afforded recognition only later to deny that it had done so. Presumably recognition of the TRNC by Islamic nations would be coupled with aid to the new country. Saudi Arabia has recently provided funding to build a new highway from Nicosia to Kyrenia.[6] But despite constant canvassing the TRNC has failed so far to win recognition from any state save Turkey, and so long as the Secretary General is prepared to pursue his mandate of good offices it seems unlikely that others will soon come forward.

There are other options for the Turkish-Cypriot section. The TRNC could become a province of Turkey, though this would be opposed by a substantial proportion of the Turkish-Cypriot community and would have adverse repercussions for Turkey internationally. It is, however, an option Ankara might be prepared to pursue, rather than accept a solution which led to substantial dilution of the concentration of Turkish-Cypriots in the north.

Denktash has said he could conceive of economic and security arrangements with the mainland rather like those which Monaco has with France. Just as the Principality has consular but not full diplomatic relations with many nations, so, too, the TRNC might seek arrangements which would facilitate the movements of its people abroad and the arrival of tourists, without the necessity for full diplomatic relations. Such an arrangement would satisfy Turkish security requirements without the diplomatic cost of direct annexation and, unless there is a political settlement which unifies the island by the end of the century, this seems the likeliest evolution.

Greece has repeatedly said that it has abandoned *enosis*. The events of 1974 demonstrated that it would not be able to defend Cyprus except at the risk of all-out war with Turkey, and the potential for losses in the Aegean and Thrace outweighs any advantages to be gained on the island. Nevertheless, Prime Minister Papandreou has implied that Greece would be prepared to fight were there any further Turkish advance in Cyprus.[7] Athens believes that as the centre of Hellenism it has 'interests' in Cyprus, and to this end it has consulted closely with the Greek-Cypriots over the course of the inter-communal negotiations and has co-ordinated its foreign policy to support the Greek-Cypriot cause. Greece has been a major contributor to the cost of supporting UNFICYP, and the socialist government has said it would provide a substantial proportion of the cost of maintaining an international force on the island if Turkish troops were withdrawn.

Until 1987, the socialist government insisted there could be no discussions with Turkey about any of the multitude of disputes which divide the two allies until Turkish troops were withdrawn from Cyprus. This policy changed, however, after the incident over Aegean drilling rights in March that year, which saw both countries put their armed forces on alert. An exchange of notes between Papandreou and Ozal led to the Davos process with its 'no war' accord and the evolution of a bilateral agenda for consultations at ministerial and heads of government level to seek confidence-building measures. This influenced attitudes on the island and played a role in the election of Vassiliou over the rejectionist Kyprianou.

Initially it appeared that in the Davos process the Greek and Turkish leaders had agreed to set aside the issue of Cyprus, but following meetings between Vassiliou and Papandreou in March 1988, Greece indicated that it would use the contacts to pursue the matter of Turkish troop withdrawals. It did this at the summit between the Greek and Turkish leaders in June of that year. The Greek emphasis on the issue soured the talks but did elicit intimations that Turkey might not be committed to a permanent military presence on Cyprus.

The disputes between Greece and Turkey in the Aegean are not a direct consequence of the situation in Cyprus, but the tension which it has engendered fuels the two nations' animosity. It was the Turkish invasion of Cyprus which triggered Greek withdrawal from the integrated military structure of NATO and spurred its reinforcement of its islands. This, in turn, redounded on the Alliance in the series of inter-related disputes over command-and-control arrangements, exercise procedures, assignment of forces, and the development of NATO infrastructure. Likewise, Cyprus has adversely affected the bilateral basing agreements which the US has with the two allies, leading to a diminution of the availability of the facilities and persistent problems for successive American administrations in securing their future. A settlement in Cyprus would not break the log-jam in this nexus of disputes but it would facilitate their resolution. Similarly, if the Davos process were to lead to reconciliation between Greece and Turkey it would give a fillip to the negotiations in Cyprus.

It is therefore in the interests of the members of the Western alliance, America in particular, to promote a settlement in Cyprus. But, as America has found to its cost, he who sticks his head above the parapet often gets shot at, and the Reagan Administration confined itself to offering economic incentives towards a settlement while monitoring the progress of the ongoing UN efforts towards that end. It is possible that the incoming Bush administration may be able to produce some fresh ideas. Certainly Turkey is more likely to give them a hearing than it would have any proposals that might have been advanced by defeated Governor Michael Dukakis who is of Greek extraction.

The UK continues to recognize the Greek-Cypriot administration as the government of the Republic and treats with representatives of the TRNC only at an official rather than a government level. It continues, however, to be the major non-Turkish trading partner of the northern territory and has blocked efforts by the Greek-Cypriots to prevent such trade being afforded preferential tariff treatment under the terms of the Cypriot Association Agreement with the EC. UK policy, conditioned by its concern for the SBAs, is to deal with the problem at one remove through the UN. This is likely to continue. The Thatcher Government has been a stronger proponent of Turkish entry into the European Community than those of many other of the 12 member states.

The European Community has been made increasingly aware of the Cyprus problem since Greek entry in 1981, the conclusion of the Customs Union Agreement with the Republic of Cyprus in 1987, and the Turkish application for full membership that same year. On past precedent, however, it is unlikely that the Community will become involved. Policy to date has been to ignore disputes between member states concerning national matters. The Community's pursuit of greater internal political cohesion in due course may change this approach, but probably not in a time-scale relevant to the Cyprus problem, unless this becomes so prolonged as virtually to preclude resolution.

Secretary General Xavier Pérez de Cuéllar set June 1989 as the target date for the conclusion of a new agreement under the latest peace initiative. At the time of writing (late 1988) there was no indication that the talks between the parties would produce a settlement by that date. Turkey must hold nationwide municipal elections by March 1989 and these will have the character of a referendum on the economic policies of the Ozal Government, while Greece must go to the polls by June 1989 in national elections in which the Papandreou Government, for reasons unrelated to Cyprus, will be on the defensive. On past form this would have impeded rather than promoted progress over Cyprus. There is, however, a faint hope – albeit no more than a glimmer – that, with the Davos process established, and with the Greek and Turkish leaders due to meet again sometime early in 1989, on this occasion the desire to enhance their political prestige by promoting some movement over Cyprus might help efforts towards a settlement.

The principal matter which must be resolved is the presence of Turkish troops on Cyprus. The Turkish-Cypriots feel that a protective force must remain and that there must be some form of guarantee whereby Turkey has a legal right of future military intervention. Deterrence by proximity is not considered sufficient. The Greek-Cypriots, for their part, demand a timetable for the withdrawal of the Turkish troops and some form of guarantee which will prevent their return.

There has been extensive debate over whether the right of unilateral action reserved to the guarantor powers was meant to include armed invasion.[8] In moral terms, Turkey may have had some justification for its first intervention in July 1974 given the poor conditions under which its Turkish-Cypriot compatriots had lived for the previous 11 years and given also the immediate threat to their safety posed by the Greek junta-sponsored coup and the installation as president of a man with Sampson's record. Turkey argues that Makarios had failed to respect the constitution by not implementing power-sharing and by curtailing the civil and human rights of the Turkish-Cypriots. It claims that the coup was an act of aggression aimed not just at dividing but at annexing the island. However, the Turkish claim that the Treaty provides the legal justification for its action is flawed. The right of unilateral action was afforded under the proviso that it be exercised to restore the constitutional *status quo*. Even Turkey's first military intervention did not purport to be doing this. The Turkish demand at the Geneva talks which followed *Attila I* was for a federal structure which had been expressly excluded from the power-sharing, but unitary, 1960 constitution.

The Treaty of Guarantee stipulated that its purpose was to prevent either union of Cyprus with any other state or partition of the island. The second Turkish invasion in August 1974 imposed *de facto* partition. Nevertheless, Turkey justifies this action by invoking the Treaty of Guarantee.

While the Greek junta of 1967–74 was intent on *enosis*, the civilian governments which have succeeded the dictatorship have repeatedly asserted that Greece has abandoned any unionist designs on the island and favours its continued independence. There are thus neither sound political nor legal reasons for the continued presence of Turkish troops on the territory of the sovereign state of Cyprus. Their presence serves only to secure Turkey's interest in maintaining a buffer state between the mainland and what once was the largest Hellenic island off its long and vulnerable coastline. Agreement to the withdrawal of these forces or, at the very least, to a timetable under which this is to be effected, is the key to resolution of the Cyprus problem.

Notes

Chapter I

[1] Richard A. Patrick, *Political Geography and the Cyprus Conflict: 1963–71*, Department of Geography Publication Series No. 4 (Waterloo, Ont: University of Waterloo, 1976), p. 3.

[2] *North Cyprus Almanack* (London: K. Rustem & Brother, 1987), pp. 17–18. Similar sorts of policies are being pursued in northern Cyprus today.

[3] Stavros Panteli, *A New History of Cyprus* (London and The Hague: East-West Publications, 1984), pp. 175–6.

[4] Cypriot forces fought, however, in both the British and Greek armies.

[5] The only residual communal vestiges were some 120,000 Greeks living as Turkish citizens, principally in Istanbul and Izmir, and 87,000 Muslims living as Greek citizens in Thrace. Other examples of the separation of peoples included the enforced exodus of the Turkish community from Crete prior to its union with Greece in 1913 and the de-Hellenization of Gökçeada and Bozcaada, two once predominantly Greek islands at the mouth of the Dardanelles, assigned to Turkey at Lausanne. For details see Christopher Hitchens, *Cyprus* (London: Quartet Books, 1984), pp. 151–3, and Alexis Alexandris, 'Imbros and Tenedos: a Study of Turkish Attitudes Toward Two Ethnic Greek Island Communities Since 1923', *Journal of the Hellenic Diaspora*, vol. VII, no. 1 (New York: Pella Publishing Co., Spring 1980), pp. 5–31.

[6] For analysis of the psychological import for the Turks of the balance struck in the Aegean by the Treaty of Lausanne, see Andrew Mango, 'Greece and Turkey: unfriendly allies', *The World Today*, vol. 43, nos. 8–9 (London: Royal Institute of International Affairs, August/September, 1987), pp. 144–7.

[7] The number of actual fighting men in the organization was miniscule. Its commander, General George Grivas, was always pointedly vague, claiming a 'mere handful' of combatants. Robert Stephens says there were probably never more than 300 men under arms at any one time. See Robert Stephens, *Cyprus:*

a Place of Arms (London: Pall Mall Press, 1966), p. 157. These fighters were organized in small action groups specializing in sabotage, execution, ambush and counteraction to Turkish-Cypriot separatist activity. However, while the fighters were few, EOKA had the tacit support and co-operation of the vast majority of the Greek-Cypriot population. Writing in his memoirs Grivas spoke of 'our invisible army which covered the whole island. . . . It was present everywhere but never showed itself. As for its numbers, it is difficult even for me to say. For, ultimately because of our system, every Greek Cypriot, from the smallest child to old men and women, belonged to our army, and fulfilled a mission either as a combatant or in the auxiliary services'. See George Grivas, *Guerrilla Warfare and Eoka's Struggle*, trans. A.A. Pallis (London: Longmans, Green and Co. Ltd., 1964). p. 10. This tiny force was confronted by some 30,000 British troops.

[8] Grivas, a native Cypriot, took Greek citizenship to join the Hellenic Army. In the wake of the liberation of Greece from the Nazis, Grivas led a white-terror campaign against communist partisans which helped precipitate the second round of the Greek civil war, 1947–9.

[9] For further discussion see Stephen Xydis, *Cyprus: Reluctant Republic* (The Hague and Paris: Mouton, 1973), pp. 87–8; and Stephens (*op. cit.* in note 7), pp. 139–40.

[10] From 1955–7, the government of Adnan Menderes in Ankara employed the slogan 'Cyprus is Turkish'. By 1957, this had been transformed into 'Partition or Death'. See Feroz Ahmad, *The Turkish Experiment in Democracy* (London: Royal Institute of International Affairs, 1977), p. 404.

[11] It was encapsulated in the slogan 'From Turk to Turk'.

[12] The literal translation is volcano, but the title was chosen for its connotation of 'eruption'.

[13] Stephens (*op. cit.* in note 7), p. 160.

[14] It was Denktash himself who revealed that he had established the guerrilla group without Küçük's knowledge. See Christopher Thomas, 'The politics of

resistance that divided Greek from Turk', *The Times*, 20 January 1978. 'I had set up the TMT . . . with a few friends to organize the individuals who were rushing around doing things. When the TMT issued its first pamphlet taking over from its predecessor, *Volkan*, Dr. Kutcuk (sic) asked who these fools were. We had not told him about TMT. He was happy with *Volkan*. He never got out of the feeling that he was left out out of it. . . . Eventually TMT became more than a military force, it became a moral force. Everybody thought I was the leader but I was not. I was political adviser. Immediately after forming it I handed it over. It was a good mask because even the British and American intelligence thought I was the man who ran and decided everything. I was not'. The leaders, he said, were former army officers from Turkey.

[15] For seven years the UK was to retain sovereignty and responsibility for external affairs, defence and internal security. For other matters, though, the British Governor would work in consultation with representatives appointed by the Greek and Turkish governments. The Greek- and Turkish-Cypriots would be given the nationality of their motherlands as well as that of the UK. A constitution providing for representative government would be drawn up in consultation with members of the communities, together with the governments in Athens and Ankara. Prime Minister Harold Macmillan stressed the need to create a sense of partnership which, in time, would lead to a peaceful transition to independence.

[16] Xydis (*op. cit.* in note 9), p. 65.

[17] Julian Amery, [Undersecretary of State for the Colonies (1958–1960) and later Under-Secretary of State for War] Testimony before the UK House of Commons Select Committee on Foreign Affairs, *Cyprus,* 3rd report, 1986–87 session (London: HMSO, 1987), p. 50.

[18] Stephens (*op. cit.* in note 7), pp. 163–7. The Greek delegation apparently believed that it had the approval of the Greek-Cypriot leadership for all the basic elements of the constitution save the clause requiring separate majorities in the House of Representatives for tax laws. This became a major issue in the impasse which led to the breakdown of power-sharing. A constitutional commission sitting on the island did consider details of the charter but was not able to change certain fundamentals which secured and guaranteed basic rights to the communities.

[19] The Maronite, Armenian and Latin Christian communities all opted to be 'Greeks'.

[20] Zaim Neçatigil, former Attorney General of the Turkish Federated State of Northern Cyprus, describes the constitution as providing for 'partnership and co-founder status of the Communities, the bi-communality of the State and the dichotomy of functions and powers between the State and the Communities'. See *The Cyprus Conflict – a Lawyer's View* (Nicosia: Tezel Offset and Printing Co. Ltd., 1982), p. 7.

[21] Philip Windsor, *NATO and the Cyprus Crisis*, Adelphi Paper No. 14 (London: ISS, November 1964), p. 3.

[22] For details see Stephens (*op. cit.* in note 7), pp. 172–4; and Keith Kyle, *Cyprus*, Report No. 30 (London: Minority Rights Group, 1984), pp. 8–9.

[23] There is a question whether the Greek-Cypriots ever intended to abide by the constitutional provisions. The Turkish-Cypriots point to a document called the Akritas Plan, allegedly prepared by Interior Minister and former EOKA gunman, Polycarpos Georkadjis, detailing a programme for Greek-Cypriot political action to modify the constitution and to abolish the Treaty of Guarantee with a view to proceeding to a plebiscite on self-determination. The document said that in the event of Turkish-Cypriot armed resistance, it was to be swiftly crushed by superior Greek-Cypriot force before the guarantor powers could act. The text may be found in Necati Ertekün, *The Cyprus Dispute* (Nicosia: K. Rustem & Brother, 1981), pp. 165–71.

[24] The changes included: abolition of the veto of the vice president and of the separate majority voting system in the House of Representatives; unification of the courts, police and gendarmerie; changes in the ratios in the civil service and the military to make them more

accurately reflect the population; and abolition of the concept of separate municipal authorities.

25 Patrick (*op. cit.* in note 1), p. 96. He says that some 350 Turkish-Cypriots probably died, together with some 200 Greeks and Greek-Cypriots. Patrick was formerly a Captain in the Canadian armed forces serving with the United Nations Force in Cyprus and his is the most authoritative account of this period by a neutral observer.

26 Accounts of the events vary widely. Field Marshal Lord Carver, the Commander of the Truce Force has written in 'Peacekeeping in Cyprus', in *Cyprus in Transition 1960–85*, John Koumoulides (ed.) (London: Trigraph, 1986), p. 22, 'both sides had armed bodies of men ready to go into action immediately: . . . the Turks had a plan, which they executed, to leave all government service, and to try and set up a parallel administration of their own, at the same time abandoning a number of mixed and isolated villages [103 according to Turkish-Cypriot sources] and concentrating their population in areas where they were less vulnerable; and . . . the Greeks had plans, which they executed with brutality and callous disregard of human life, to drive Turks out of certain areas, particularly in the northern suburbs of Nicosia, where their presence was either an embarrassment or a real threat to Greeks'. Yet Robert Stephens has written '. . . neither the suggestion of a carefully planned Turkish rebellion nor that of a systematic Greek attempt at extermination or terror will bear close examination. Despite their clandestine activities, both sides were ill-prepared militarily and politically when the clash came. Nor had either side taken the elementary precautions which should have been evident if they had been preparing for battle, such as the removal of their compatriots from unsafe areas. It was not until after the fighting had begun that the Turks began to move out of some of the mixed villages and to concentrate in the Nicosia area, either voluntarily or from fear or, in some cases, under pressure from the Turkish leadership. The same is true of the Greek evacuation from some areas where they were outnumbered and in danger'. Stephens (*op. cit.* in note 7), p. 101.

27 George Ball, *The Past Has Another Pattern* (New York & London: W.H. Norton, 1982), p. 342.

28 Windsor (*op. cit.* in note 21), pp. 17–18.

29 Resolution 186, 4 March 1964.

30 The letter said 'a military intervention in Cyprus by Turkey could lead to a direct involvement by the Soviet Union. I hope that you will understand that your NATO allies have not had a chance to consider whether they have an obligation to protect Turkey against the Soviet Union if Turkey takes a step which results in Soviet intervention without the full consent and understanding of its NATO allies'. The full text and Inonu's response appear in *The Middle East Journal*, Number 20, summer 1966, pp. 386–93.

31 See among others: Van Coufoudakis, 'US Foreign Policy and the Cyprus Question: An Interpretation', *Millenium: Journal of International Studies*, vol. 5, no. 3 (London, 1977), pp. 248–9 and 266; Andreas Papandreou, *Democracy at Gunpoint* (New York: Doubleday & Co. Inc., 1970), p. 137; Theodore Couloumbis, *The United States, Greece and Turkey: The Troubled Triangle* (London: Praeger, 1983), p. 47; and, Laurence Stern, *The Wrong Horse, The Politics of Intervention and the Failure of American Diplomacy* (New York: Times Books, 1977), p. 84.

32 The Karpasian peninsula and the Bögaz region in the north-east.

33 The Acheson scheme went through several modifications in the course of the summer's negotiations, including a proposal that the Turkish sector in Cyprus be held on a 50-year lease and another that Greece should cede a larger island such as Chios or Samos.

34 Papandreou (*op. cit.* in note 31), p. 140.

35 'The 1960 Constitution of the Republic of Cyprus and the Doctrine of Necessity (CPS/102). Supplementary Memorandum by the Government of the Republic of Cyprus, in *op. cit.* in Ch 1, note 17) pp. 91–4.

36 This is the generally accepted figure.

Patrick (*op. cit.* in note 1) gives the figure of 5,000. Papandreou (*op. cit.* in note 31) says 20,000.

37 Patrick (*op. cit.* in note 1), p. 68.

38 *Ibid*, pp. 83–6.

39 When he returned clandestinely in 1967, he was arrested and ignominiously deported to Turkey.

40 Patrick (*op. cit.* in note 1), p. 86. According to Patrick, '. . . The relationship between [the general] and the ambassador was unclear; most certainly it could not be assumed that [he] was subordinate to the ambassador. In matters where civil and military considerations overlapped, there was close liaison between the General Committee and senior Fighter officers. Questions which were not resolved at this level were subject to mediation, arbitration or direction by the Turkish embassy or even by the Turkish government. In such instances, weight was given to considerations of security'.

41 Galo Plaza, *Report of the United Nations Mediator on Cyprus to the Secretary General*, S/6253 (New York: United Nations, 26 March 1965).

42 The affair was murky and involved allegations by Grivas that Papandreou's son, Andreas, had become involved in a conspiracy with left-wing army officers in a cabal known as *Aspida* (shield). When the elder Papandreou sought to take over the Ministry of Defence which was to conduct an investigation, King Constantine refused. George Papandreou resigned and a constitutional crisis ensued when the monarch, instead of accepting Papandreou's demand for fresh elections, tried on three occasions to form governments based on splinter groups from the Centre Union party. After two months of political unrest, Papandreou's former Deputy Prime Minister, Stefanos Stefanopoulos, formed a minority administration with the support of the conservative opposition. It was expected to last only a few weeks in office but managed, by various devices, to hang on to power until December 1966, when it was brought down after Papandreou and the conservative leader Panayotis Kanellopoulos made a pact with the monarch to hold fresh elections in May 1967. These were pre-empted by the

Colonels' *coup d'état*. The alleged rationale of the participants in the coup was the need to reform the old political order to create parties of principle rather than personality. Many political figures, particularly those on the left, believe the two-year political crisis was engineered by the Greek intelligence agency, with CIA connivance, in order to secure a government more compliant to the partition of Cyprus.

43 Ioannis Toumbas, *From a Minister's Diary* [private translation from the Greek] (Athens: Filon, 1986), pp. 149–51.

44 BBC, *Summary of World Broadcasts*, (hereafter *SWB*) ME/2447/C, 21 April 1967, p. 4.

45 See Polyvios Polyviou, *Cyprus, Conflict and Negotiation, 1960–1980* (London: Duckworth, 1980), pp. 122–4.

46 Miltiades Christodoulou, *The Progress of an Era* [private translation from the Greek] (Athens: Ioannis Floris, 1987), pp. 492–3.

47 For details of the incident see Michael Harbottle, *The Impartial Soldier* (London: Oxford University Press/RIIA, 1970), pp. 145–67. Harbottle is a former commander of UNFICYP. Grivas has given conflicting reasons for mounting the attack. On the one hand, he claimed to be acting on orders from hard-liners in the military regime in Athens, and on the other he has said that he was acting on the orders of Makarios who was seeking to destabilize the situation on the island in order to get rid of the Greek forces which had been infiltrated onto Cyprus. Neither explanation rings entirely true.

48 He was assisted by interventions from a special envoy of the UN Secretary General, José Rolz-Bennett, and NATO Secretary General, Manlio Brosio.

49 Zaim Neçatigil, *Our Republic in Perspective* (Nicosia: Tezel Offset and Printing Co. Ltd., 1985), pp. 10 and 13.

50 Polyviou (*op. cit.* in note 45) p. 128. He says the accord was due in large part to 'NATO mediation'.

51 EOKA-B fighters were also involved in the coup. However, the role of that organization had grown increasingly ambiguous. Grivas died of natural causes in January 1974 while still in the field conducting clandestine operations

against the Makarios Administration.
The degree of his estrangement from the
policies pursued by Athens was
illustrated by the fact that the man he
nominated as his successor was Major
George Karousos, a former Greek army
officer who for a time had been detained
by the dictatorship for his involvement
in an underground resistance movement
against the Colonels' regime.
[52] Taki Theodoracopulos, *The Greek
Upheaval* (London: Stacey International,
1976), pp. 35–6.
[53] There are numerous accounts of the
coup. Among the more graphic are
Theodoracopulos (*ibid*); C. M.
Woodhouse, *The Rise and Fall of the
Greek Colonels* (London: Granada,1985);
and Stern (*op. cit.* in note 31).
[54] Turkish-Cypriot sources compare the
action to that of the UK in Ulster,
America in Grenada, and India in Sri
Lanka. According to several Turkish
authorities, Ecevit had ordered the
troops not to fire unless fired upon and
this is why the first wave was contained
in such a small area. See, e.g., Mehmet
Ali Birand, *30 Hot Days* (Lefkosa: K.
Rustem, 1985), p. 15. The
Greek-Cypriots dismiss this suggestion
out of hand. Certainly violent Turkish
propaganda posters of the time bore no
hint of any concept of restraint.
[55] *Ibid*, p. 7.
[56] James Callaghan, *Time and Chance*
(London: Collins, 1987), p. 340.
[57] There are several published accounts,
among the best being Stern (*op. cit.* in
note 31) and Woodhouse (*op. cit.* in note
53).
[58] This followed UN Security Council
Resolution 353 of 20 July 1974. The
Turkish troops, however, continued
openly to expand their bridgehead until
30 July 1974 when it formed a rough
triangle between northern Nicosia and
points 10 kilometres to the east and west
of Kyrenia.
[59] There are several published accounts,
among the most detailed being
Callaghan (*op. cit.* in note 56) and
Birand (*op. cit.* in note 54).
[60] Callaghan *ibid*, p. 348.
[61] This was the generally accepted figure
in the press at the time. Turkish sources
say only 20,000 troops were landed.
[62] Greece also approached the UK with

a view to joint action under the Treaty
of Guarantee. A division was ordered to
be mustered in Crete with tanks and
other heavy equipment, and the UK
government was asked to provide air
cover for it to sail to Cyprus.
Karamanlis proposed to travel with the
force, together with his defence minister
Evangelos Averoff. In a private
interview, the latter said they would
have been prepared to fight if they met
resistance. Prime Minister Harold
Wilson took two days to respond, by
which time the ceasefire had been
declared. See C.M. Woodhouse,
Karamanlis (Oxford: Clarendon
University Press, 1982), p. 218.
[63] The then Foreign Minister, George
Mavros, who later went on to lead the
opposition Centre Union party, has said
in a private communication that he
considers the decision to have been
'both too hasty and too late . . .; too
hasty because it was not preceded by a
clear warning which may have made a
difference and too late because it
followed *Attila II* [the assault plans were
codenamed *Attila I* and *II*] and could
therefore no longer make a difference'.
[64] Carl Barkman, *Ambassadeur in
Athens. Van Dictatuur tot Democratie,
1969–1975* (The Hague: Staatsuitgevery,
1984).
[65] Stern (*op. cit.* in note 31), p. 95.

Chapter II

[1] Communique issued at the end of the
third round of inter-communal talks
under UN auspices in Vienna from 31
July to 2 August 1975. The text may be
found in Ertekün, (*op. cit.* in Ch I, note
23), p. 257.
[2] The communique said specifically that
'Greek Cypriots at present in the north
of the island are free to stay and that
they will be given every help to lead a
normal life, including facilities for
education and for the practice of their
religion as well as medical care by their
own doctors and freedom of movement
in the north'.
[3] *Report by the Secretary General on the
United Nations Operation in Cyprus
1 December 1987 to 31 May 1988*,
S/19927 (New York: United Nations, 31
May 1988), p. 13.
[4] The estimated population in 1986, the

last year for which official figures are available, was 677,000. The last formal census was in 1960 when, out of a total population of 577,615, there were 442,251 Greek-Cypriots (80 per cent) and 104,350 Turkish-Cypriots (18 per cent) with the remaining 30,744 inhabitants consisting of Armenians, Maronites and Latins. An unofficial census in 1970, after the constitutional requirement that all citizens declare themselves to be Greek- or Turkish-Cypriots, indicated that there were 518,617 Greek-Cypriots (82 per cent) as opposed to 114,383 Turkish-Cypriots (18 per cent). The Turkish-Cypriots allege that over the course of years the Greek-Cypriots have granted citizenship to 100,000 mainland Greeks. They further claim that as many as 250,000 Turkish-Cypriots live abroad in mainland Turkey, the UK and elsewhere, having left the island as a consequence of the troubles.

[5] The authorities have declined to produce statistical evidence.

[6] A leading Turkish-Cypriot journalist, who favours the present state of affairs but who, like many Turkish-Cypriots, objects to the influx of mainlanders, estimated the figure to be as high as 85,000. He spoke unattributably. Western embassies accept a figure of 30–35,000.

[7] Turkish-Cypriots of left-wing political persuasion say that economic necessity has forced many of their number to quit the island as a majority of jobs are in the gift of the administration, which has been dominated by conservatives, and they have had difficulties in obtaining employment.

[8] This only came into being formally after the 1983 declaration of independence.

[9] Resolution 3212 (XXIX), 1 November 1974.

[10] Dentkash has said that Turkish-Cypriots hold title deeds to some 30 per cent of the privately owned land of the island, though this is at odds with the 1960 census which showed they held just over 20 per cent. (In 1977, the Greek-Cypriots claimed this figure had been reduced to 16.7 per cent.) Denktash also claims that the Turkish-Cypriots, as co-founders of the republic, are entitled to half the lands in the public domain which constitute some 28 per cent of the total territory of the island (26.3 per cent according to the Greek-Cypriots).

[11] He did have to take account of the continued presence of EOKA-B which, while nothing like as active as before the coup, did not disband until after his death.

[12] Resolution 367, 12 March 1975.

[13] Ertekün (*op. cit.* Ch I, note 23), p. 278.

[14] Neçatigil (*op. cit.* in Ch. I, note 20), pp. 219–28.

[15] *Ibid*, pp. 229–41.

[16] Ertekün (*op. cit.* in Ch I, note 23), pp. 357–9.

[17] *Ibid*, p. 360.

[18] Private communication. The text is sketchy and contains a number of potential ambiguities.

[19] BBC, *SWB*, ME/6888/C, 24 November 1981, p. 3.

[20] In an interview with *The Times*, 17 May 1983, Denktash argued: 'We have discovered that the world recognizes societies which call themselves states and their governments. Anyone not using that title is disregarded, rejected and condemned on the basis of what people who call themselves governments put before them. My proposal to my people will be – and I shall stand by it whatever may happen – to declare that in the north a Turkish-Cypriot government exists and will seek recognition as the northern state, a sovereign state, open to further discussions with the southern state of Mr Kyprianou for establishing the federation.'

[21] *Quarterly Economic Review of Lebanon, Cyprus*, 1/84 (London: Economist Intelligence Unit, 21 February 1984), p. 14.

[22] *Report by the Secretary-General on the United Nations Operation in Cyprus 10 December 1985 – 11 June 1986*, S/18102 Add. 1 (UN Security Council: New York, 11 June 1986), p. 3.

[23] *Ibid*, p. 2.

[24] *Ibid*, pp. 13–17.

[25] The potential problem as perceived by the Greek camp was summed up by Andreas Papandreou in a statement to the European Council at The Hague in June that year.

'The Turkish Cypriot leader leaves no doubt that all Turkish troops will not be withdrawn. . . . As regards the timetable, Mr Denktash could not be clearer. First, the present government of the Republic of Cyprus will be dissolved. Then a transitional government will be formed, whose powers of action will be non-existent because of the Turkish-Cypriot right of veto, which features heavily in the draft Framework Agreement. The dissolution of the Cypriot National Guard will follow. And only then, when the legal government of the Republic of Cyprus no longer exists, when the Greek-Cypriots are defenceless in the face of about 30,000 Turkish troops of occupation, will the withdrawal of such Turkish forces as will finally leave begin. If any one of us faced such a situation in his own country, I wonder if you would react any differently from President Kyprianou.'

26 Quoted in Pérez de Cuéllar (*op. cit.* in note 22), p. 21.

27 BBC, *SWB*, ME/8302/C, 4 July 1986, p. 1.

28 Turkish officials say Denktash requested this document as a basis for discussion because it was indicative of the progress of the negotiations flowing from the 1979 high-level meeting and not because he agreed with the 4:2 ratio of representation mentioned therein. They add that the March 1986 text has not been dropped and that it still 'has its uses'.

Chapter III

1 A Legislative Council presided over by the British governor and composed of nine appointed British officials plus 15 elected Cypriots – 12 Greek-Cypriot and three Turkish-Cypriot – functioned from 1925–31. The Council proved divisive because whenever the matter of *enosis* was raised the Turkish-Cypriots aligned themselves with the colonial power to defeat Greek-Cypriot interests. All representative institutions were dissolved in 1931 following violent Greek-Cypriot protests for *enosis*. Municipal councils were revived in 1943.

2 He took 67 per cent of the popular vote, less than might have been expected, given the way in which he dominated the *enosis* struggle. He was opposed by the Democratic Union under John Clerides, the father of Glafkos. Clerides was a moderate who believed that the power-sharing arrangements set out in the constitution would not work. He was backed, on the one hand, by hardline unionists who believed the acceptance of independence under any guise compromised their cause and, on the other, by AKEL who believed that ex-EOKA men were too influential in Makarios' government.

3 Two lawyers who formed a left-of-centre party and published a newspaper advocating closer association between the communities were murdered by TMT gunmen in April 1962. Ordinary citizens were harassed to quit organizations such as trade unions and co-operatives which transcended communal lines.

4 Yiannis Roubatis, *Tangled Webs* (New York: Pella Publishing Co. Inc., 1987) pp. 135–7. He says the US urged the British authorities to pay more attention to the party and its activities.

5 Kyriacos Markides, *The Rise and Fall of the Cyprus Republic* (New Haven CT: Yale University Press, 1977), p. 61.

6 Xydis (*op. cit.* in Ch. I, note 9), p. 43. He says this decision was part of a 'Gentleman's Agreement' between Prime Ministers Constantine Karamanlis and Adnan Menderes which was not published. See also Markides, *ibid*, pp. 59–66 and 80–81.

7 The Unified Front, headed by Clerides, took 15 seats. The Progressive Front, which embraced Sampson and other right-wing conservatives, won seven. AKEL, despite voting strength estimated to be in excess of a third of the electorate, confined itself to contesting nine seats, winning them all. The Socialist Party (EDEK) took two and independents two.

8 Markides (*op. cit.* in note 5), p. 33.

9 In addition to those discussed here, there are the Centre Union (*Enosi Kentrou*) headed by Tassos Papadopoulos, a former EOKA leader and sometime inter-communal negotiator, and the Liberal Party (*Komma Phileleftheron*) headed by Nicos Rolandis who served as foreign minister under Spyros Kyprianou until breaking

with him over the president's refusal to sign the Secretary General's draft agreement in New York in January 1985.
[10] The Socialist Party, the National Democratic Union of Cyprus. Its leader, Dr Vassos Lyssarides, was personal physician to Makarios and thus had regular access to the Ethnarch. Lyssarides claims to have been the 'spiritual father of Cypriot non-alignment'. See T. W. Adams, *AKEL: The Communist Party of Cyprus* (Stanford, CA: Hoover Institution Press), pp. 144–7.
[11] Ostensibly Sampson was freed on licence to travel abroad to undergo treatment for a chest complaint and was supposed to return to Cyprus to complete his sentence. He remained overseas. It is generally agreed that by this means the government had got rid of a potential opposition rallying focus. Sampson would have been eligible for parole as early as 1984.
[12] Initially 0.5 per cent, it had, by 1988, been increased to two per cent.
[13] Greece has been the fourth largest contributor to UNFICYP after the US, the UK and the Federal Republic of Germany. Turkey, by contrast, has been well down the list, with contributions standing at about a tenth of Greek levels.
[14] Former Prime Minister George Rallis has described it as 'a very grave error'. He implies that the settlement plan formed part of a package whereby Greece would abandon its Congressional lobby to maintain the US arms embargo on Turkey – which had led to the closure of US bases there – in exchange for America pursuing with vigour the implementation of a settlement. 'The Cypriots could have discussed the plan with the Americans and sought improvements on its substance. If they didn't achieve that, they would at least have an excuse for rejecting the plan. . .'. *Hours of Responsibility* [private translation from the Greek] (Athens: Euroekdotiki, 1983), pp. 316–7.
[15] On 6 December 1985 Papandreou said in a parliamentary debate in Athens that 'We must tell the Cypriot people clearly that if they agree to a timetable for the withdrawal of Turkish troops – which means Turkish troops will never withdraw – we will consider Greece's

national interest is being harmed'. At the heart of the debate within the Greek camp at the time was whether they should insist on Turkish troop withdrawals prior to a settlement or agree to a timetable for their withdrawal as part of the implementation of an agreement.
[16] 'The Peoples' Army'. See Adams (*op. cit.* in note 10), p. 145.
[17] In a joint public statement issued late in 1987, the Communal Liberation Party, the Republican Turkish Party and the People's Thrust Party charged that '. . . State Offices have been rendered functionless. Official decisions are being taken at National Unity Party headquarters'. The declaration alleged, among other things, that members of opposition parties seeking employment in the administration were first required to resign, that trade unionists were being coerced to quit the left-wing *Dev İş* trade union movement and that the opposition press was being denied public advertisements, thus depriving it of a vital source of revenue. See *Friends of Cyprus Report* [Newsletter], No. 30 (London: Friends of Cyprus, Autumn 1987), pp. 3–4.
[18] As well as the major parties discussed here, other parties currently in operation include the Democratic People's Party (*Atilimci Halk Partisi*), a nationalist social democratic party created by former members of the National Unity Party; the Working People's Party (*Çalişan Halkin Partisi*), an extreme left-wing party; the Cyprus Democratic Party (*Kibris Demokrasi Partisi*), a left-of-centre breakaway from the Communal Liberation Party; the Northern Cyprus Socialist Party (*Kuzey Kibris Sosyalist Partisi*) which favours complete independence; the Social Democratic Party (*Sosyal Demokrat Parti*) which favours a federal republic; and the New Turkish Unity Party (*Yeni Türk Birligi Partisi*) an extreme right-wing party.
[19] This is also translated variously as the Renaissance Party and the New Dawn Party.
[20] For a number of years in the late 1970s, the party had the support of Dr Küçük's influential newspaper *Halkin Sesi*. But this had more to do with the

former community leader's personal grievances against Denktash than with any positive support for Communal Liberation Party. During this critical 1981 election Küçük threw his weight behind the UBP.

[21] Özker Özgür, head of the CTP, claims that when Turkish Foreign Minister Ilter Turkmen arrived in Cyprus to oversee the efforts to form a government, he made it clear that the policies of the CTP were unacceptable to Ankara. The party was sufficiently left-wing that it would have been banned on the mainland under the military dictatorship then prevailing. For the TKP and CTP to form a working coalition they needed the support of the two members of the Democratic People's Party, of which one was the former UBP prime minister, Neçat Konuk. He was so opposed to the idea of entering into a coalition with the left-wing Republican Turkish Party that he resigned from the Democratic People's Party thus eliminating the possibility of an opposition coalition securing a majority in the House. Özgür claims Konuk was persuaded to do this by Inal Batu, the Turkish ambassador. The Communal Liberation Party, on the other hand, believes that he acted out of friendship for Denktash.

[22] 'Politics in the North', *Friends of Cyprus Report*, [Newsletter] No. 23 (London: Friends of Cyprus, Winter 1981/82), pp. 5–7. This is one of several comprehensive articles on Turkish-Cypriot politics; others appear in issues 19, 26 and 27. They have an anti-Denktash bias.

[23] For example, three members were included from *Turk Sen*, the trade union federation affiliated with the Western-oriented International Confederation of Free Trade Unions, while no places were given to *Turk Iş*, the workers' federation affiliated to the Eastern bloc's World Federation of Trade Unions.

[24] BBC, *SWB*, ME/8355/C, 4 September 1986, p. 1.

[25] 'Turkish Cypriots Establish a New Regime in North', *International Herald Tribune*, 24 May 1988.

[26] BBC, *SWB*, ME/7466/C, 17 October 1983, p. 2.

[27] The acrimony between Özgür and

Denktash has degenerated to a personal level. In January 1988, the president won a libel case against the CTP leader and was awarded TL 200 m in damages (subsequently reduced to TL 80 m on appeal). A procedure was set in train to lift Özgür's parliamentary immunity from prosecution on the grounds that he had committed a crime against the state by insulting the president. A committee of the Legislative Assembly voted that it should be lifted but, according to Özgür, did not report its decision to the House because of international pressures. He claims that an effort to seize the presses of the party newspaper, *Yeni Duzen*, in lieu of the damages was prevented only when party members threw a human chain around the printing works.

[28] Özgür contends that the party could still be dissolved if it pursues the federalist line too vehemently. Article 71/1 of the constitution provides that 'The rules, programmes and activities of political parties shall not violate the indivisibility or the integrity of the State. . .'.

Chapter IV

[1] Nicos Vassiliou, *The Widening Economic Gap* [pamphlet] (Nicosia, undated), p. 2. The Turkish-Cypriots note that they abandoned some 40 per cent of the island's vineyards in the south.

[2] *Country Profile, Cyprus* (London: Economist Intelligence Unit, 1988), pp. 50–51. Many of the figures appearing here are taken from this publication. Other sources include: *Annual Report for 1986* (Nicosia: Central Bank of the TRNC, March 1987), and *Statistical Yearbook for 1985* (Nicosia: State Planning Organisation Statistics and Research Department, December 1986).

[3] In constant 1980 prices.

[4] *Economic and Social Developments in the Turkish Republic of Northern Cyprus* (Nicosia: State Planning Organisation, 1 September 1987), p. 1.

[5] In constant 1977 prices. According to the State Planning Organisation the number of manufacturing units doubled from 230 in 1974 to 460 in 1985.

[6] State Planning Organisation (*op. cit.* in note 4), p. 3.

[7] The exchange rate in 1980 was TL 75 = $1. Early in 1988 it stood at TL 1,236

=$1. The Cyprus pound remained legal tender until 1983 but since has been treated as a foreign currency. It remains the favoured black market currency in preference to both sterling and dollars.
[8] At the then prevailing rates of exchange.
[9] 'Profile Cyprus', *European Energy Report*, No. 257 (London: Financial Times Business Information, 12 January 1988), pp. 8–11.
[10] The Turkish-Cypriots nonetheless bill northern consumers. Officials say this supports the cost of maintenance of the grid in the north and the production of the northern input to the system.
[11] The first EC financial protocol in 1977 provided Ecu 30 m, the second in 1983, Ecu 44 m and the third was expected to be around Ecu 60 m.

Chapter V

[1] The Greek agreement dates from 1953, the Turkish from 1954. Many of the facilities were held on 99-year lease. The first US tactical air squadrons were stationed in Turkey and Greece in 1955 and 1958 respectively. Details of the bases and their roles may be found in Congressional Research Service, *US Military Installations in NATO's Southern Region*, a report prepared for the Subcommittee on Europe and the Middle East of the Committee on Foreign Affairs of the US House of Representatives (Washington, DC: US Government Printing Office, 7 October 1986), pp. 31–54.
[2] It has been publicly acknowledged that the US base at Inçirlik in south-eastern Turkey was used during the American landings in Lebanon in 1958 and that US aircraft flew supplies from Adana to Amman to support King Hussein against the Palestinians in 1970. Communications, stores and port facilities in Greece remained open to the US during the 1973 Arab–Israeli war, though direct combat and logistic support was ruled out by both Greece and Turkey. However, the former US ambassador to Greece, Monteagle Sterns has implied that America may have exceeded national constraints on its use of the bases. In 'The Aegean Triangle', a monograph due to have been published by the Wilson Center in November 1988. He writes: 'Restraints placed by Greece and Turkey on our ability to use military facilities on their territory in Middle Eastern contingencies are the result of American troop movements and resupply operations through Hellenikon and Inçirlik air bases in 1958, 1967 and 1973 about which the host countries were not consulted'.
[3] UK Parliament, House, Select Committee on Cyprus, *Report* session 1975–76 (London: HMSO, 8 April 1976), p. 63.
[4] Roubatis, (*op. cit.* in Ch III, note 4), pp. 134–5. Makarios reportedly received $1 m a year to allow the bases to continue. The funds were reportedly not paid to the Cypriot exchequer but channelled via the church into welfare work.
[5] Xydis (*op. cit.* in Ch I, note 9), p. 345.
[6] Couloumbis (*op. cit.* in Ch I, note 31), p. 90.
[7] *Ibid*, p. 51.
[8] Allegations have been made that the CIA used the Greek dictatorship to channel funds to Richard Nixon's 1968 election campaign. See Seymour Hersh, *Kissinger: The Price of Power* (London: Faber and Faber, 1983), p. 137; and Hitchens (*op. cit.* in Ch I, note 5), pp. 125–30.
[9] During the Colonels' tenure there were the two Arab–Israeli wars, Colonel Gaddafi seized power in Libya and King Hussein acted to drive out dissident Palestinians from Jordan, a move which ultimately destabilized Lebanon. Terrorism, particularly aircraft hijacking, was rife throughout the Mediterranean basin.
[10] The agreement provided anchorages for six American destroyers at Elefsis Bay and involved the use of the Athens area as the home base for their crew and dependents. Negotiations for a homeport for one of the carriers had not been completed when the dictatorship fell.
[11] See, for example, Laurence Stern, 'Bitter Lessons: How we failed in Cyprus', *Foreign Policy*, no. 19 (Washington, DC: Carnegie Endowment for International Peace) Summer 1975, p. 41 and 48–9; and, chapters 14 and 15 of Stern, (*op. cit.* in Ch I, note 3).
[12] See, for example, John Cooley, 'New Cyprus plot thwarted'; *Christian Science*

Monitor, 14 August 1973.

[13] Assistant Undersecretary of State Sisco was authorized ultimately to threaten removal of nuclear weapons from Thrace and Anatolia if there was no cease-fire. See Henry Kissinger, *Years of Upheaval* (London: Weidenfeld and Nicolson, 1982), p. 1,192 and Callaghan (*op. cit.* in Ch I, note 56), p. 345.

[14] Stern (*op. cit.* in Ch I, note 31), p. 131 and Birand (*op. cit.* in Ch I, note 54), pp. 96–8. It would have given them political control over 34 per cent of the territory of the island instead of the 37 per cent finally taken. Callaghan does not mention this compromise and implies that Turkey insisted throughout on a bizonal settlement.

[15] Kissinger (*op. cit.* in note 13), pp. 1,191–2. According to British historian C.M. Woodhouse, himself a former intelligence officer, a NATO report at the time indicated movements of Soviet military aircraft and special forces into Balkan countries. (*op. cit.* in Ch I, note 62), p. 217.

[16] Callaghan (*op. cit.* in Ch I, note 56), pp. 351–2.

[17] For details see Andrew Wilson, *The Aegean Dispute*, Adelphi Paper No. 155 (London: IISS, 1979).

[18] Thanos Veremis, 'Greece and NATO: Continuity and Change', in John Chipman (ed.) *NATO's Southern Allies: Internal and External Challenges*, (London: Routledge, 1988), p. 269.

[19] *Ibid*, p. 272. Turkey claims the airfields at Chios and Kastellorizon also could take military aircraft.

[20] Wilson (*op. cit.* in note 17), p. 40.

[21] Ton Frinking, *Interim Report of the Sub-Committee on the Southern Region of the North Atlantic Assembly Political Committee*, AB206 (Brussels: International Secretariat, 1984), pp. 29–30. A comparable description was provided to the author by the Turkish General Staff.

[22] Wilson (*op. cit.* in note 17), p. 16.

[23] Royal Decree of 4 April 1937, *Official Gazette, A*, No. 146, 21 April 1937.

[24] Both sides have published extensive pamphlet literature under the imprint of ostensibly neutral organizations. The Greek case has been set out in *Threat in the Aegean* (Athens: Journalists' Union of the Athens Daily Newspapers,

undated); *The Legal Status of Lemnos* (Athens: Hellenic Institute for Defense and Foreign Policy, 1987); *The Status Quo in the Aegean* (Athens: The Institute for Political Studies, undated). The Turkish case appears in *The Aegean Realities* (Istanbul: The Association of Journalists, undated) and *Turkish-Greek Relations Disputes and Arguments*, a mimeographed booklet with no publication details, distributed by the Turkish General Staff. The author's observation is based principally on discussions with Greek and Turkish diplomats and NATO officials at Supreme Headquarters Allied Powers Europe (SHAPE).

[25] The author's comments are based on briefing by the Hellenic National Defense General Staff. For an assessment see Veremis (*op. cit.* in note 18), pp. 270–3.

[26] In an interview at the time, George Rallis, then Minister to the Prime Minister, and later successor to Karamanlis, said 'We'll not send our troops back if first we do not find a satisfactory solution on Cyprus. We insist that we must find a solution in Cyprus which will be accepted by the Greek Cypriots and will also be a solution that won't compromise Greek national prestige. It's not blackmail. It's a necessity for us. Our allies must help to put pressure on the Turks to find a solution.'

[27] Previously there had been two joint commands at Izmir in Turkey – Allied Land Forces Southeastern Europe (LANDSOUTHEAST) and the Sixth Allied Tactical Air Force (SIXATAF) – each under a US general with Turkish and Greek deputies. With the withdrawal of the Greek officers in 1974 these became effectively Turkish operations and when the tours of duty of the senior US officers ended, command was assumed by Turkish generals with US deputies.

[28] During the Cyprus hostilities Turkey issued a notice to airmen (NOTAM) requiring all aircraft approaching Turkey to report their position and flight plan on reaching the median line. Greece refused to acknowledge this and responded with its own NOTAM declaring Aegean air routes to be unsafe. This precluded all flights between

Greece and Turkey and required that other civil air traffic fly around the disputed area, a situation which prevailed for six years.

[29] It baulks, however, at Greek suggestions that this might be reciprocal, with the Greek air force providing air cover over the Dardanelles from Lemnos.

[30] An unofficial text believed to be accurate may be found in Robert McDonald, 'Alliance Problems in the Eastern Mediterranean – Greece, Turkey and Cyprus: Part II,' *Prospects for Security in the Mediterranean*, Part I, Adelphi Paper No. 229 (London: IISS, Spring 1988), p. 87.

[31] Papandreou told parliament on 6 December 1985 that true 'equidistance' would be to include Lemnos in exercises one year and not the next. *SWB*, ME/8131/C, 11 December 1985, p. 4.

[32] As a consequence of the various disputes, Allied Command Europe (ACE) has not staged any reinforcement exercises in Greece since 1974. Nor does Greece contribute to the Naval On Call Force, Mediterranean (NAVOCFORMED). It does, however, continue to participate in the NATO Air Defence Ground Environment (NADGE) and the NATO Airborne Early Warning Force (NAEWF) which it sees as serving national interests.

[33] Turkey bases its case on the Chicago Convention on Civil Aviation of 1944 which says that national airspace extends to the limit of territorial waters. Since the question of extension of the Greek six-mile territorial limit is central to the dispute in the Aegean, it refuses to accept the ten-mile airspace.

[34] *The Times*, 17 April 1976.

[35] Congressional Research Service, *US Military Installations in NATO's Southern Region, Report for the Subcommittee on Europe and the Middle East of the Committee on Foreign Affairs of the US House of Representatives,* 99th Congress, 2nd Session (Washington, DC: USGPO, 7 October 1986), p. 349.

[36] *Ibid*, p. 351.

[37] In September 1988, the Greek government advised the US that if a new agreement were achieved Hellenikon airbase, which provides support for USAFE and the Military Airlift command and a base for electronic and photographic reconnaissance missions, would have to be closed. The government said its functions could not be relocated elsewhere in Greece.

[38] *International Herald Tribune,* 28 March 1987.

[39] Papandreou insists that it is not a 'non-aggression pact'.

[40] The agreement calls for both parties to respect each other's rights, sovereignty and territorial integrity, and at the same time to respect rights to use the open seas and airspace. They undertook to avoid obstructing normal shipping and air traffic during military exercises in international waters and airspace and to abide by international rules. They further agreed not to hold exercises in the Aegean during the peak holiday season, 1 July – 1 September, and, if it was found necessary to close an exercise area, they agreed that it should not 'isolate certain areas' and that the duration should be limited. Both sides have postponed exercises at the other's request as a result of the agreement.

[41] The projects which were allowed to proceed were a Turkish low-frequency broadcast station on the Dardanelles and a Greek fast patrol boat base on Skyros.

[42] *SWB*, ME/0253/C, 10 September 1988, p. 1.

[43] *Cf.* Richard Haass, 'Alliance Problems in the Eastern Mediterranean – Greece, Turkey and Cyprus: Part I', *Prospects for Security in the Mediterranean*, Part I, Adelphi Paper No. 229 (London: IISS, Spring 1988), pp. 69–70. Several of the measures adopted by Greece and Turkey are similar to proposals advanced in this Paper.

[44] *Financial Times*, 16 June 1988.

[45] *Ibid.*

[46] The UK government contracted to provide £12 m sterling in aid to the new republic in 1960–65 but there was no linkage to the bases. Spending associated with their presence contributes substantially to the Cypriot economy. In 1987 purchases of supplies and services plus servicemen's outlays were estimated to total £59 m sterling, two per cent of Greek-Cypriot GDP.

47 Residual controls were retained over Nicosia airport pending consolidation of flight services within the base areas. The UK has continued to be sensitive about the airport area and moved forces there under UN colours during the Turkish advance in 1974.

48 Select Committee on Cyprus, *Report*, (*op. cit.* in note 3), pp. 63–4, para. 208.

49 In 1979, it was suggested that the base might be used to house US reconnaissance jets monitoring Soviet compliance with SALT II.

50 Select Committee (*op. cit.* in note 3), p. 53–4, para. 136.

51 *Ibid*, p. xxx, para. 11.

52 Carver (*op. cit.* in Ch I, note 26).

53 Minister of State at the Foreign and Commonwealth Office Roy Hattersley, (*op. cit.* in note 3), p. 15, para 5. See also Carver (*op. cit.* in Ch I, note 26), pp. 36–7, and Callaghan (*op. cit.* in Ch I, note 56), p. 356. There were some 8,800 British servicemen on the island: 5,000 serving with the RAF at Akrotiri, 3,000 with the army at Dhekelia and 800 with UNFICYP. In *Attila I* Turkish forces put ashore just 6,000 men with 30 tanks under air cover. The UK authorities argued, however, that, despite British troop numbers, they could not have prevented the Turkish landing because few of their forces were combat troops and they had only armoured cars and no appropriate air cover.

54 Callaghan (*op. cit.* in Ch I, note 56), p. 340.

55 Ministry of Defence (*op. cit.* in note 3), pp. 88–9.

56 See *The Daily Telegraph*, 24 July 1974; and Callaghan (*op. cit.* in Ch I, note 56), p. 347.

57 *The Daily Telegraph*, 1 April 1988.

58 For a more detailed discussion of Soviet policy towards Cyprus and relations between the Soviet Communist Party and AKEL, see Adams (*op. cit.* in Ch III, note 10), pp. 158–71.

59 In the 1974 coup the National Guard used Soviet T-34s which Makarios had purchased from the USSR.

60 See Duygu Bazoğlu Sezer, *Turkey's Security Policies*, Adelphi Paper no. 164 (London: IISS, Spring 1981), pp. 23–4.

61 *On the principles of a Cyprus settlement and ways of achieving it*

(proposals of the USSR), 21 January 1986.

62 Andriana Ierodiakonou and Edward Mortimer, 'Papandreou softens line on Turkish EC quest', *Financial Times*, 21 May 1988. '...Dr Papandreou said there was 'absolutely no question' but that Greece would back Turkey if the Cyprus issue were solved. 'If the troops go, that for me would be sufficient', he said. 'I think it would be such a great event, to have the removal of the occupation of Cyprus, that Hellenism I think would say yes'. ... He added, however, that 'Cyprus as a country may have other conditions, notably a timetable for the departure of 60,000 mainland Turkish settlers from northern Cyprus, and adequate international guarantees for the permanence of the settlement.'

Chapter VI

1 *Human Rights and Cyprus*, 2 vols., Turkish Cypriot Human Rights Committee of the Turkish Federated State of Cyprus, January 1977.

2 European Commission of Human Rights, *Report of the Commission on Applications Nos 6780/74 and 6950/75 by Cyprus against Turkey* (Strasbourg: Council of Europe), adopted 10 July 1976, declassified 31 August 1979.

3 Nancy Crawshaw, 'Cyprus: The Political Background', in Koumoulides (ed.) (*op. cit.* in Ch I, note 26), p. 11.

4 Theodoracopoulos (*op. cit.*, in Ch I, note 52), p. 89.

5 Beginning in 1977, these have comprised, at various times, Afghanistan, Bangladesh, Djibouti, Iran, Malaysia, Pakistan, Saudi Arabia, Somalia and Uganda.

6 By comparison Kuwait has been investing heavily in the south.

7 In a foreign-policy debate in Parliament on 24 May 1987, Papandreou commented, 'If Turkey is prepared to go to war over the legal extension of our territorial waters, then why should we not be prepared in case there is an attempt to occupy the whole of Cyprus?' *SWB*, ME/8578/C, p. 2.

8 See, for example, Sir David Hunt, 'Three Greek islands and the Development of International Law', in Koumoulides (ed.) (*op. cit.* in Ch I, note 26), pp. 38–53.

Chronology

1959	Zurich and London Agreements (Treaties of Establishment, Guarantee and Alliance)
1960	16 August – Cyprus becomes an independent state; UK withdraws to SBAs.
1963	Late December – Inter-communal fighting
1964	NATO intervention proposed and rejected; 14 March– UNFICYP arrives on Cyprus; Summer – US intervention: Johnson letter to Turks, Acheson plan.
1965	Report of UN mediator Galo Plaza.
1967	21 April – Colonels' dictatorship installed in Greece; September – talks between Greece and Turkey fail to produce a solution; November – Greek-Turkish confrontation, defused by American intervention.
1968	Inter-communal negotiations begin on Cyprus.
1970	Attempted assassination of Archbishop Makarios.
1971	Turkish military *pronunciamiento*; Athens–Ankara try to impose Cyprus settlement through inter-communal talks.
1972	Attempt by Greek Colonels to unseat Makarios.
1973	Rauf Denktash elected vice president superseding Dr Fazil Küçük as leader of Turkish-Cypriot community; November – Greek Military Police Chief, Ioannides, overthrows original junta leaders, installs regime taking hard line on Cyprus.
1974	15 July – Greek-backed coup against Makarios; former independence guerrilla gunman, Nikos Sampson, installed as president, Archbishop escapes abroad; 20–22 July – *Attila I*, first Turkish intervention; 23 July – political government restored in Greece under Karamanlis; Glafkos Clerides replaces Sampson as temporary Greek-Cypriot leader; 25–30 July – First round of Geneva talks between the tripartite guarantors, UK, Greece and Turkey; 9–14 August – Second round of Geneva talks among guarantors plus the Greek- and Turkish-Cypriots; 14–16 August – *Attila II*, Turkish invasion of Cyprus; September – Autonomous Cyprus Turkish Administration created in occupied northern territory; December – Makarios returns to Cyprus.
1975	February – declaration of Turkish Federated State of Cyprus (TFSC) in occupied territories; US arms embargo applied against Turkey for misuse of aid weaponry in Cyprus invasion (lifted September 1978).
1977	February – Makarios–Denktash high-level agreement; August – Makarios dies, Spyros Kyprianou succeeds as President.
1979	May – Kyprianou–Denktash high-level meetings and expanded agreement.
1980	September – Generals seize power in Turkey.
1980–3	251 sessions of inter-communal talks.
1981	Turkish–US DECA signed; October – the socialist movement, PASOK, comes to power in Greece under Andreas Papandreou.

1983	Greek–US DECA signed; November – dictatorship in Turkey ends with surprise election of Turgut Ozal; 15 November – declaration of independent Turkish Republic of Northern Cyprus (TRNC).
1985	January – Abortive Kyprianou-Denktash high-level meeting in New York.
1986	March – Draft Framework Agreement presented by UN Secretary General.
1987	March – Greek-Turkish confrontation over oil rights in the Aegean.
1988	January – Davos *rapprochement* between Papandreou and Ozal; February – George Vassiliou elected as President of the Republic of Cyprus replacing Kyprianou; August – preliminary meeting between Vassiliou and Denktash in Vienna; September–October – talks in Cyprus; November – Vassiliou-Denktash meet with UN Secretary General in New York.
1989	March – Second tripartite meeting scheduled between Vassiliou, Denktash and UN Secretary General.

Glossary

AHP	*Atilimci Halk Partisi* (Progressive People's Party)
AKEL	*Anorthotikon Komma Ergazomenou Laou* (Progressive Party of the Working People)
CHP	*Çalişan Halkin Partisi* (Working People's Party)
COMAIRSOUTH	Commander Allied Air Forces Southern Europe
CTP	*Cumhuriyetçi Türk Partisi* (Republican Turkish Party)
DCA	Defence Co-operation Agreement
DECA	Defence and Economic Co-operation Agreement
DIKO	*Dimokratiko Komma* (Democratic Party)
DISY	*Dimokratikos Synagermos* (Democratic Rally)
EDEK	*Sosialistiko Komma, Ethniki Dimokratiki Enosi Kyprou* (Socialist Party, the National Democratic Union of Cyprus)
enosis	union
EK	*Enosi Kentrou* (Centre Union)
EOKA	*Ethniki Organosis Kypriou Agoniston* (National Organization of Cypriot Fighters)
EOKA-B	Version of EOKA revived in 1971
Halkin Sesi	Voice of the People
KDP	*Kibris Demokrasi Partisi* (Cyprus Democratic Party)
KKK	*Kommounistikon Komma Kyprou* (Cyprus Communist Party)
KKSP	*Kuzey Kibris Sosyalist Partisi* (Northern Cyprus Socialist Party)
KP	*Komma Phileleftheron* (Liberal Party)
KTP	*Kibris Türktür Partisi* ('Cyprus is Turkish' Party)
LANDSOUTHCENT	Allied Land Forces Southern Central Europe
LANDSOUTHEAST	Allied Land Forces Southeastern Europe
Mücahit	Fighters
NADGE	NATO Air Defence Ground Environment
NAEWF	NATO Airborne Early Warning Force
NAVOCFORMED	Naval On Call Force, Mediterranean
PASOK	*Panellinio Sosialistiko Kinima*
SBA	British Sovereign Base Area
SDP	*Sosyal Demokrat Parti* (Social Democratic Party)
taksim	partition
TFSC	Turkish Federated State of Cyprus
TKP	*Toplumcu Kurtuluş Partisi* (Communal Liberation Party)
TMT	*Türk Mukavemet Teskilati* (Turkish Resistance Organization)
TRNC	Turkish Republic of Northern Cyprus
UBP	*Ulusal Birlik Partisi* (National Unity Party)
UNFICYP	United Nations Force in Cyprus
Volkan	Volcano
YDP	*Yeni Doğus Partisi* (New Birth Party)
Yeni Duzen	New System
YTBP	*Yeni Türk Birligi Partisi* (New Turkish Unity Party)